GOD OR CAESAR

BOOKS BY VARDIS FISHER

GOD OR CAESAR

The Writing of Fiction for Beginners

By

VARDIS FISHER

"First listen, my friend, and then you may shriek
and bluster."—ARISTOPHANES

"Exclamation of the author upon him!"—LIUTPRAND

THE CAXTON PRINTERS, LTD.
CALDWELL, IDAHO
1953

ACKNOWLEDGMENTS

The material in this book from the works of Thomas Wolfe is used by permission of Mr. Edward C. Aswell, administrator of the Wolfe estate; and the material from the works of James Branch Cabell by the gracious permission of its author.

INTRODUCTION

NOBODY IN my opinion can teach anybody how to write creatively. One learns to write by writing and by becoming as quickly as one can one's own best critic. But there may be a few things which older writers can tell their younger fellows to help them along—to strengthen their moral will, to disabuse their minds of illusions, even if they cannot teach them the craft. In any case there are some things set down in this book which I was a long time learning and which I wish I might have learned while young.

There are no final answers here to any questions; there is only the substance and color of one author's prejudices and views. Many of those views are not, as the reader will soon discover, orthodox. Moreover, they are set forth in quite general terms, because in generalizing, said Professor Caird, we liberate truth "from the accidents of its temporary embodiment." Or we can try to: the liberation is not an easy task. Speaking of Eratosthenes, Draper says that he "hoped to free history as well as geography from the myths that deform it, a task which the prejudices and interests of man will never permit to be accomplished." Possibly not, but it is good to make the assault upon them. As far back as the records go man has devoted a great part of his energy to the suppression of truth, and still, with unabated zeal, or desperation, strives to conceal those unpleasant recognitions which knowledge steadily presses upon him. If this book does anything at all toward liberating the truths about writing from the myths which contain them I shall have to feel, quite naturally, that I have somehow accomplished a miracle.

In a book like this I think one should call without coyness or apology on one's own experiences, because we speak most authoritatively at those points where we have been severely tried. At the same time I have wished, without letting this become a mere book of quotations, to introduce the opinions of many whose credentials none can question. That I have chosen with bias let no one doubt. That I have placed my emphasis and my sympathy with those writing for God rather than for Caesar is equally plain. In extenuation it may be said that most of the books published on this subject have been intended for the latter, and for them it is doubtful whether anything could be added to what has already been said.

TABLE OF CONTENTS

PART I

GOD OR CAESAR

ARE YOU A WRITER?

"In the resistance of the will in allowing what is
distasteful to come into the illumination of the intellect lies the place where insanity can break into
the mind."—SCHOPENHAUER

"How long have you sat already upon your misfortune? Give heed! lest you hatch an egg, a
basilisk egg of your long travail."—NIETZSCHE

"Two types of artist: that which creates from
an inner need and that which does so from an inner
surplus."—RANK

IN ADDRESSING myself to those who wish to write or
who may now be in their writing apprenticeship I think
of Thoreau's traveler who came to a swamp and asked a
boy standing by if it had a bottom. On being told that it
had the wayfarer plunged in and sank to his neck. "I
thought you said this has a bottom!" he shouted at the boy.
The boy replied: "So it has, but you haven't got to it yet."

I do not expect to get anywhere near the bottom of this
subject, on which so many able minds have exercised their
faculties; but for all that I intend to speak as one ac-
credited. If you will hear me out you may then shriek and
bluster. Like Bulwer's Mainwaring we shall both need, you
and I, "the luxury—yes, the luxury—of candor"; for without it this book would be only another academic treatise
and you would be wasting your time. So let's be frank.
The first question to ask yourself is whether you have the
stuff of a writer in you. The answer, if it is to be worth
anything at all, will demand extraordinary candor. I am
here speaking to those who wish to create. Rank[1] traces
the urge to create to a "basic principle of which the general
form may be stated as the gradual freeing of the individual
from dependence." But even in the life of one who is
genuinely creative, creative acts, says Toynbee, are rare

---

[1] Otto Rank, *Truth and Reality.*

events. That may be so if Toynbee had in mind creative
acts of compelling significance; but in many people there
is a wish and a need to alter their environment. If creativeness is not primarily the altering of environment its
significance eludes me. I should think that art, a difficult
term to which we shall come later, is a result of an effort
in the artist, largely subconscious, to place a part of himself beyond the reach of death. But as his egoistic pre-
tensions and hungers are brought more and more under the
scrutiny of his mind, as with an Epicurus or a Stendhal,
it is likely that death will become less terrible to contem-
plation, and that his drive toward some sort of personal
immortality will wane, along with his creative energies.
That is all Herbert J. Muller can mean when he says that
emotional maturity would have been the death of Thomas
Wolfe. Full emotional maturity would be the death of any
artist. Lecky tells us that Marcus Aurelius, "following an
example that is ascribed to Pythagoras, made it a special
object of mental discipline, by continually meditating on
death, and evoking, by an effort of the imagination, whole
societies that had passed away, to acquire a realized sense
of the vanity of posthumous fame." If an artist were to
come to that realized sense he would be through as an
artist. Elsewhere, with the Stoics still in mind, Lecky
speaks of "pride, which looks within, making man seek
his own approbation, as distinguished from vanity, which
looks without, and shapes its conduct according to the
opinions of others." It is pride and not vanity on which
the artist must rest.

Rank views three levels—and mark them well. The first
and most superficial type "accepts reality with its demands
and so adjusts his own individuality that he perceives and
can accept himself as a part of reality." With such persons
writing can never be art. The third and highest type
accepts only his inner ideal formations and "seeks to adjust
the environment and the fellow man to himself." Creative
activity reaches its highest level "when the individual creates from himself and his own idealized will power a world
for himself." The first type depends on the appearance of
reality engendered by his prejudices, illusions and wishful
thinking; the second type, which he calls the neurotic,
tries to defend itself against reality; the third breaks
through to freedom, and so outgrows and abandons the
obsolete elements in myth, which are the anchor of the

first type and the exasperating problem of the second. In the sphere of consciousness he distinguishes three levels: the Apollonian which said know thyself; the Dionysian which said be thyself; and Kant's which said determine thyself from thyself. The first keeps his fantasies secret, the second represses them, and the third affirms them as the truth of his being. The third "creates a whole world in his own image, and then needs the whole world to say 'yes' to his creation." This type saves himself from the "neurotic chaos of will denial and self consciousness" by breaking through to his ideal formations and affirming his own creative will. That is, he breaks out of the prison of his neurosis, escapes from the blight of self-consciousness and guilt-feelings.

If you wish to be a serious writer you are neurotic, which means above all that you have feelings of guilt. If you continue to be neurotic you will be, says Rank, the "failed artist." He thinks the neurotic suffers "fundamentally from the fact that he cannot or will not accept himself." On the one hand he criticizes himself to excess, on the other hand he overidealizes himself, "which means that he makes too great demands on himself and his completeness." Though Sadger, Stekel and others have identified the neurotic with the artist, Rank believes that the artist ceases being neurotic when he breaks through to his own affirmations. There is truth in what he says but we should not push it too far.

Many experts of one kind and another—psychologists, neurologists, criminologists—have made studies of great artists of the past. W. R. Brain, a British neurologist, has concluded, for instance, that some artists of the past were insane enough to have been proper institutional cases. Well, and so are some today. Among those who were psychotic or obsessed or alcoholic or addicted to drugs he mentions Baudelaire, Flaubert, Goethe, Rousseau, Poe, Strindberg, Donne, Swift and Samuel Johnson. Swift, he thinks, was infantile. Johnson was obsessed with death. Still more recently the late psychiatrist and neurologist, Abraham Myerson, has given his opinion of a few artists in a posthumous book. Balzac, he thought, was hypomanic. Beethoven, "the prince of musicians, was quarrelsome and unreasonable"— but how few have not been! Some were epileptics. Goethe, he thinks, was a manic depressive, but Reik, it seems to me, saw him more clearly. Newton was a schizophrenic. Poe's father was a psychopath and so, he believes, was Tolstoy. And so on: one could fill a book with similar opinions.

Graham Greene thinks that every "creative writer worth our consideration . . . is a victim: of man given over to an obsession." This obsession, he believes, is a writer's motivation, his drive, and it dictates everything he does as a creative artist. Further, in all serious writers, he believes, there at some time occurs a moment "when the dominant theme is plainly expressed, when the private universe becomes visible even to the least sensitive reader." There may be, and I personally think there is, truth in what Greene says, but he goes much too far when he imagines that the core of the artist becomes visible "even to the least sensitive reader." It took a lot of doing to bring the core of Goethe into view for a psychologist as perceptive as Reik.

Whether or not the artist is obsessed it is true, I think, that he has strong feelings of guilt, and therefore tends to magnify and exalt himself. Wolfe was a notable instance of this, as we shall see in later pages. Rank believes that the artist never wholly surrenders himself to life, and that also would seem to be true; and further—this I also accept— that the more strongly a person feels his freedom and independence, or his need of them, the more intensely he is conscious of guilt. That is the basis of the old doctrine of atonement, of at-one-ment, which the Jews felt above all other people because more than any other people they broke away into an exclusive cult, taking on themselves the burden of "separateness." These problems of dependence and guilt are resolved, in Rank's opinion, when the artist breaks through to his own affirmations and establishes himself firmly within his own fantasies, myths and ideals. That is one thought to keep in mind.

Guilt consciousness is simply, as he points out, a consequence of "increased self-consciousness, yes at bottom it is just this in its most fateful working out as conscience."[2] As for the neurotic, with his tormenting burden of guilt feelings, we must recognize that he represents "not a form of illness but the most individualistic" being of our time, the affirming artist alone excepted. In the neurotic, awareness of sin and guilt, or the oppressive sense of these in the subconscious mind, makes the person unhappily self-conscious in his relations with life and his fellows. The neurotic type, to which in some degree all sensitive persons belong, "suffers

---

[2] Edward Carpenter says it better in *Pagan and Christian Creeds.*

from the fact that he cannot accept himself, cannot endure himself and will have it otherwise." He must be transformed from a negative person of guilt and suffering to a positive person of will and action. The "passive man of suffering cannot act because his self-consciousness restricts his will which manifests itself as guilt feelings in the face of the deed." As in psychic sexual impotence, for instance. The neurotic will solve his problem when he finds his own truths. It is to be regretted that Rank did not explore the origin of guilt feelings and neurosis in certain doctrines of ancient Judaism and Pauline Christianity, which have had such immense influence in shaping the Western world.

Very well, then, you are neurotic. You suffer from feelings of guilt or you would have no wish to be a serious writer. You were born with a certain degree of intelligence to which you can never add an iota. Heredity fixed that. Your childhood discovered and shaped your major interests; these you can hope to direct but never to abandon. Your egoism has been overdeveloped; this can be your strength or your fatal weakness, depending on how you manage it. "What are we all doing from morning to night," asked Kingsley, "but setting up our own fancies as the measure of all heaven and earth, and saying, each in his own dialect, 'When it pleases heaven to open your eyes you will see as I do.' "

In no other field are persons so convinced that they are the servants of heaven. In no other field are they so likely to be. Overdeveloped egoism and feelings of guilt produce both the prophet and the poet. Because of his inner creativeness, the artist, Rank says, is antireligious, in the sense that his ambition is "always subservient to the individual desire for immortality in the creative personality and not to the collective glorification of the creation of the world." Which means that the true artist is always a heretic. He tries to save his individuality from the collective mass by stamping his own personality upon his work. This tendency to immortalize himself and to establish himself as his own supreme being is so powerful in him that he is forever "seeking to protect himself against the transient experience, which eats up his ego." Or to find the universal in the particular. If convinced that he has failed in this he is likely to kill himself or go insane. His egoism is so extreme that whether philosopher, painter, sculptor or writer he does not wish to teach his pupil his doctrines but "to transform

him into his own image." Keep that in mind when you come
to what is said about writers' conferences and courses in
creative writing.

The genuine artist is always a heretic. Let us pause a
moment here to see what has been said about that. There
is, Gide has said, "no true work of art without the collabo-
ration of the Devil." "Without the Devil," said James
Huneker, "there would be no art." Indeed, in the Middle
Ages all art was thought to be the work of the Devil! "I
have heard all the men of letters say that their profession
was diabolical," Delacroix tells us; and Gottfried Keller,
the novelist, has put it this way: "He who has had no
bitter experiences knows no malice; and he who has known
no malice has not the Devil in him; and he who has not
the Devil in him can not write anything that will have
force and vigor." Of Milton, William Blake said: "The
reason Milton wrote in fetters when he wrote of angels and
God, and at liberty when of devils and hell, is because he
was a true poet, and of the Devil's party without knowing
it." And Boehme found the downfall of Satan in his wish
to be an author.

If the artist does not understand the sources of his
neurosis there is pretty sure to be in him too much Jeremiah
and not enough Ruth; too much of Ezekiel and too little
of the Preacher; too much of the evangelist, too little of the
poet. He may become the helpless prisoner of his self-
protective illusions. He may nourish deep in his private
chambers the notion that he is a great and misunderstood
genius born out of his time. "It is the proud consciousness
of certain qualities," said Bulwer, "that it cannot reveal
to the everyday world, that gives to genius that shy and
reserved and troubled air which puzzles and flatters when
you encounter it." It is more likely to be, as the perceptive
Stendhal recognized, a wish to copulate with your mother,
or hatred of your father, or something else but similar that
gives you that shy and troubled air. I would eschew the
word genius. It is a word that has been worked to death
in this country, which has taken all superlatives as its
special right. The word goes back of course to the ancient
notion that every person had an attendant spirit, a kind
of tutelary deity, which protected him and promoted his
interests. Even a psychologist now and then, as for instance
Lipps, argues that genius is a gift from above. Dessoir
found the truth when he called it the subconscious mind.

Talent is enough if you have enough of it. Persons with talent, said Hegel, are those who force mankind to discuss and explain them, including of course the impostors. To force mankind to discuss and explain you is exactly what you want to do.

You feel that in a special way you are very precious. At the same time, it is to be hoped, you are harassed and goaded by doubt—by doubt of your capacity and powers and worth. If you have no such doubts this book is not for you. If you have such doubts take comfort in Pater's thought that the way to perfection lies through a series of disgusts. Remember with Rolland that life for the artist is a series of deaths and resurrections. Bear in mind with Royce that the soul that has never doubted does not know whether it believes, that "the thinker who has not long dwelt in doubt has no rights to high rank as a reflective person." It is so easy, said Arnold, in his fine essay on Wordsworth, "to feel pride and satisfaction in one's own things, so hard to make sure that one is right in feeling it!" But also bear in mind with Professor Barzun that "so-called established writers who after years of work still wince at criticism are certainly not established in their own souls." Yet how many do not wince?

Let's glance at Hemingway in the now famous or notorious (one of his admirers has called it a horrendous caricature and he himself has called it a disaster) *New Yorker* profile (May 13, 1950). There you will find egoism and doubt in the most naked conflict. There you see his fear that he may not be a great writer after all, even while he places himself (according to Lillian Ross) above all novelists but Tolstoy. Even while he cries out that he was "champion" in his twenties, again in his thirties, again in his forties, and then recently in his fifties, doubts rise to challenge him. There is revealed, almost too painfully, his morbid fear of age and death; his scorn of formal education and of erudition even while he shows pride in the fact that he had a son at Harvard; and his obsession with the jargon of fighting and killing, in which alone he seemed able to express himself. It may indeed be a horrendous caricature but it is also a pitiless revelation of an artist's soul.

Strong doubt is of course only the other side of overdeveloped egoism. Nature strives constantly to maintain a balance. In one moment Balzac cried: "My tragedy shall become the breviary of kings and nations. I intend to make

my debut with a masterpiece or break my neck." But again:
"My distress springs from the fact that I realize how little
talent I possess." The person completely sure of himself
when he is up is likely to be a sad spectacle when he is
down. You should have faith and doubt: they nourish one
another. And you should keep always in mind Sarah
Bernhardt's words: "Intelligent people make egoism a
virtue; fools make it a vice."

You can have too much faith or too much doubt. If you
are obsessed with the thought that you are, potentially, a
great writer you may have only the image of yourself which
you see in a mirror. On the other hand your problem may
be one of despair. In writing of Liszt's symphonic poems
Wagner said, "I will hold by my experience that whoever
waits for recognition by his foes, before he can make up his
mind about himself, must have indeed his share of patience,
but little ground for self-reliance." That is not necessarily
true. There have been writers with more confidence in
their powers than powers to confide in. There have also
been writers whose childhood problems have been so extreme as to defeat their talents. You must of course
believe in the worth of what you are doing; but if you
believe so deeply that you have no tormenting doubts you
may as well tear down your ramparts and abandon your
towers. The logical goal for the person with no doubt of
himself is paranoia. The position to find, if you can manage
it, is that nice balance between the two extremes, that
will allow neither to tyrannize over the other or to be in-
different to the other's presence.

If you have come with me to this point without too
much outrage of your self-esteem I must assume that you
have come with candor. We now approach a matter that
will demand all the courage and candor you have. Let's
start off gently with the famous story about Arlen and
Ferber when they met in Paris. According to the version
in my notes Miss Ferber said: "Why, Mr. Arlen, you look
a little like a woman!" And Arlen retorted: "My dear
Miss Ferber, so do you—a little." The artist is a kind of
hybrid, half-man and half-woman, half-woman and half-
man. You have only to look at the photographs of most
of them to perceive that. I do *not* have homosexuality in
mind.[3] Real homosexuals are rare, even if homosexual

---

[3] On the homosexual diathesis in contemporary literature see the series of articles
in *The American Mercury* in 1950.

practices may be commonplace. I have in mind what psychologists call cross-identifications—that is, identifications in childhood with the opposite sex. With what fury and pain young writers resist knowledge of this! Some have come to me, seeking nourishment of their ego while pretending to seek advice. All with one exception have been furiously outraged and in most instances have fled when I told them they were as much woman as man, as much man as woman. Stendhal, with his insatiable self-searching, had far greater candor; he said the reading of *The Prince* was a "good remedy for that instable sensitivity which makes me like a woman, and is disguised only by my facility for reasoning." One young man went out in such fury that I could hear him babbling to himself as long as he was in sight. I mean of course in your responses to situations, in your sensibilities, yes, and I hope even in your tenderness. There are few things of which young writers need a clearer apprehension than of this in themselves— and I suggest that you read Dr. Hinkle's essay which is mentioned in the last chapter. It would also be well to become familiar with the profound psychological truths in the bisexual gods of ancient times. It is a matter of common observation that most male artists are rather effeminate, and female artists rather masculine, in their appearance, but this is of little consequence. Some artists are very feminine or masculine in appearance, like Millay and Hemingway. But those who try to understand Hemingway will fail until they realize that his nature is essentially feminine. It is not for nothing that he has devoted so much of his life to guns, war, and killing.

The fact that if man there is so much woman in you, if woman, so much man, is your most precious endowment. How much less artist you could be if you were all one or the other! It is largely because you are both that you are neurotic, confused, frustrated and rebellious. It is this that fills you with an urge to alter your environment, or, as Rank puts it, to break through to willing and affirming. Your discontent, said Tolstoy, is something to thank God for. "A cleavage between life and the form in which it has to be lived is the genuine sign of a true life, the precondition of all that is good." You have many reasons to be unhappy. The demands placed on persons by the dogmas of the Christian churches to insure "salvation" are so antagonistic to the development of the individual's powers

that protest subconsciously takes many forms, including
insanity and suicide. Many young writers contemplate
suicide. They should understand that suicide can be, and
in the case of certain writers of the recent past obviously
has been, a last bitter and outraged rejection, not only of
the doctrine of original depravity but of the whole theo-
logical apparatus of at-one-ment, devised to restore persons
to an imagined original purity. Suicide in such instances,
the psychologists tell us, is an effort to preserve what is
left of the ego, to place it beyond the reach of the transient
experiences that are absorbing and destroying it. Some
writers when psychically blocked turn to Hindu mysticism,
as Huxley did; some turn to communism to find their god
there; and some like Eliot and Waugh and Auden retreat
to a moribund church. After pointing out that Auden dismissed Wolfe's fiction as grandiose rubbish, Herbert J.
Muller, possibly with a touch of malice, reminds us that
Auden "has returned to the doctrine of original sin" which
is as "false to the actual complexities and paradoxes" of
life as the opposite view of natural goodness. Of course
it is. When the artist is driven back to some ancient ego-
shelter he has largely ceased being an artist with significance if not for his time at least for the future.

Your egoistic over-development means that you are over-
motivated. It is your over-motivation which more normal
people have in mind when they speak of your offensive
egoism. In other words you are aggressive, you have
"drive." The under-motivated person may be richly en-
dowed with talent—there have been notable instances—
but he will not or can not bring his talent to fruition. He
may be a schizoid, like a brilliant poet-friend of mine who
appears to have given up. This sort is not compelled with
enough strength and singleness of purpose to prove, not
only to others but to themselves, and even more there, that
they are not the abject and meaningless creatures which
in childhood they felt themselves to be. It is not, as Wagner
put it, a matter of foes—that sounds too much like Wolfe
and Balzac. "I have genius," wrote Wolfe, "and I shall yet
force the inescapable fact down the throats of the rats
and vermin who wait the proof!" "I shall rule unchal-
lenged," wrote Balzac, "in the intellectual life of Europe! . . .
I shall stride on over the heads of all those who wanted to
fetter my hands and hinder my advance! Under persecution
and injustice my courage has grown hard as bronze."

Such stuff is adolescent nonsense. You have no right to expect your superiors to accept you as proved until you are proved.

Knowledge is virtue, said the ancient Greeks. Evil comes from ignorance, a truth so obvious that the world's long indifference to it can be ascribed only to that fondness for error which fear begets and self-esteem nourishes. You will take one of two directions: toward self-discovery or toward escape into the self-protective illusions. "By an odd fate," said Anatole France, "the very metaphysicians who think to escape the world of appearance are constrained to live perpetually in allegory. A sort of poets, they attack the colors of the ancient fables, and are themselves but collectors of fables. Their output is mythology, an anemic mythology without body or blood." We shall see what he means when somewhere in these pages we look briefly at Cabell.

The judgment may seem severe. It is true nevertheless that two world wars in one generation, the dissolution of Christian dogmas,[4] and the abandonment in intellectual circles of the supernatural have been forcing some writers to re-examine old avenues of escape or old forms of ego-enhancement. Whether they flee into mysticism or the Church or into that exhumed ancient emperor worship known as communism, or into sheer unintelligibility, it is clear enough that they choose flight to self-searching, some primitive form of nirvana to frank acceptance of the rational position which it appears that mankind will have to accept or perish. They do become collectors of fables, and their disciples and cultists do enshrine them.[5] It takes no prophet to foretell that their fables and their cults will eventually have no interest for anyone but the literary antiquarians.

The more deeply you explore yourself the more you will be enriched by that precious value which psychologists call empathy. The more fully you understand the common humanity of all people—I would say with the ancients of all forms of sentient life—their frailties and lusts, nobility and courage, cowardice and meanness, and the loneliness in their living and striving, the greater artist you may hope to be. When you meet a person, Schopenhauer advised,

[4] On this see Prof. Richard W. Boynton's *Beyond Mythology*.

[5] I have recently read that Auden's cultists lovingly gather all the "master's" remarks, even the most casual, and publish them in the literary quarterlies.

"do not consider his bad will, his narrow understanding in perverse ideas; as the former may easily lead you to hate and the latter to despise him; but fix your attention only upon his sufferings, his needs, his anxieties, his pains." Then, he said, you will feel sympathy and kinship.

That is in sharp contrast to the view expressed by the late Albert Jay Nock. In his account of himself as a superfluous man he tells of a discussion he had with the architect, Ralph Adams Cram. Then he goes on to say that it was Cram's thesis, which he accepted, that the vast majority of human beings do not behave like human beings for the simple reason that they are not. "We have accepted them as psychically-human, dealt with them on that assumption, and expected a corresponding psychical reaction, when actually nothing of the sort is possible. They are merely the sub-human raw material out of which the occasional human being is produced." When, said Nock, he perceived this truth, to him so palpable, he found himself "quite unable either to hate anybody or to lose patience with anybody . . . one can't hate sub-human creatures or be contemptuous of them, wish them ill, regard them unkindly." And so "for the first time really" he came to like people-at-large, somewhat in the way that he was fond of a dog. Cram and Nock were, of course, right, but Nock's pity rather than hate of the evil which the sub-human creatures produce sprang from that elegant snobbery which characterized him. Still, you will do well when looking at people to keep Mr. Cram's thesis in mind.

Sympathy is a broader and less exact term than empathy. Empathy, as I understand it, means that one feels one's way into another person's situation and *realizes* it, not with one's own complex of ideas, prejudices and beliefs, but with his. We can't do it very fully but we can try to do it. This, after all, may be the creative writer's great and (I should say, almost) sublime function. The artist doesn't belong to himself. He belongs to his talent and his talent belongs to the race. Empathy and understanding go hand in hand; they beget and nourish one another; and out of their union comes that "universal" perspective which Goethe thought to be the chief criterion of significant art.

A story tells us that when the ambassador from the French court presented to the Buddhist King of Siam a request from Louis XIV that he become a Christian, the King replied: "It is strange that the King of France should interest himself so much in a matter which concerns only God, whilst He whom it does concern seems to have left it wholly to our discretion. Had it been agreeable to the Creator that all nations should have the same form of worship, would it not have been as easy for Him in His omnipotence to have created all men with the same sentiments and dispositions, and to have inspired them with the same notion of the true religion?" That is another thought to keep by you.

In feeling yourself into the situation of another you will depend largely on your intuitive processes. Intuition is another obscure and rather meaningless word; as I use it here it means the presence in our conscious life of the forces, powers and discriminations of the subconscious mind. Rank, for reasons that elude me, tends to belittle the importance of the subconscious in creative activity, while at the same time approving Schopenhauer's belief that all people in their dreams are poets of the stature of Dante and Shakespeare! "The might of artistic creation," says Reik, "is so great that unintentionally, and even against its will, it reveals to the psychologist things no textbook can tell him. The metaphors of the poet are often more meaningful than technical scientific language with all its precision and clarity. The psychologist is perforce content if he succeeds in expressing the processes of the unconscious approximately...."

We know that the wealth stored under the level of consciousness does come up into consciousness in various ways. It comes up in our dreams, in hypnosis, in unconscious writing, in free associations, and sometimes in embarrassing missteps in speech and gesture. The creative writer, I am convinced, uses chiefly his subconscious mind. This must be so: the subconscious is the storehouse of memory and knowledge. People no doubt vary widely in the degree and the manner in which their subconscious mind directs their conscious activity. It can hardly be supposed that anyone is uninfluenced by that mind. I take it to be true that the more creative the person, the more active the subconscious mind is likely to be. In some forms of insanity the conscious mind abdicates and the person is delivered into the custody of his deeper mind.

We don't know much about that mind. We have not as yet contrived any satisfactory way to explore it. That some day we shall goes without saying. As well as I've been able

I have for a long time observed the interplay in myself of the two minds, and for me I am sure that no other study could be more fascinating and rewarding. And for the artist I should think that none is more indispensable.

Here is one of the many instances which I could offer. When, in laying out a novel, I thought of the protagonist's name as June I wondered whence the name had come and what unknown associations had impelled me to choose it; and during the composition and afterward I was troubled by a sense of having known this woman in the flesh. Long after the book was published there came one day, in one of those flashes from the subconscious which unknowing people interpret as mystical, memory of this woman. Some years before writing the novel she had been one of my students. I was startled to realize that, though consciously I had forgotten her, I had in my book faithfully described her physical appearance and mannerisms, and had used some of the stories about herself which she had told me. Her name was June. Maugham has confessed that he must have in mind an actual person before he can "invent" one. With some writers it may not be necessary to have an actual person in mind, but I suspect that an actual person is always the source of any successful characterization.

"We shall be wise," wrote John Cowper Powys, "if we recognize, before it is too late, that the thing most sacred in us is that strange margin of unoccupied receptivity, upon which settle, in their flight over land and sea, the beautiful wild birds of unsolicited dreams." That statement appealed to me immensely when I was young. Now I recognize it as the pretty fancy of a mystic; but mysticism, we may asume, is housed and nourished in that mind below the conscious level. I would put the matter less poetically. I would say that this we know: mystics and ecstatics and "spiritists" draw, in ways largely if not wholly unperceived by them, from their buried storehouse. We know that problems can and do descend, with sleep or exhaustion, to that mind, and that solutions of the problems are sometimes given forth to consciousness. We know that strange intimations of future events, of having lived before, and of similar mystic and mysterious revelations, come from that mind, though in ways that are still obscure and baffling. If we ever succeed in exploring it fully and in understanding its processes, the supernatural as a concept will take its place with ghosts. If you wish to explore your subconscious mind I know of no better way than to read, in the minutes before falling asleep, something that deeply disturbs you, and then to recall and examine your dreams.

In fiction Joyce has of course made the most determined, and some think the most successful, effort to explore it. Though we must accord full justice to the magnificence of his effort, we have no good reason to accept it as more than a tour de force, or to imagine that it will not some day be looked back upon as a pretty fumbling attempt to explore an area that is still too dark for our lanterns.

You should get on terms as intimate as possible with your subconscious mind. For the most part you will write out of it, if you are creative, with your conscious mind again and again doing little more than to formulate your phrases. The conscious mind, says a popular author who has written on this subject, is not big enough to write a novel. That is literally true, if by novel you mean something with significance. I do not want to sound mystical; my position on mysticism is similar to that of the author of *Folkways*. But I have learned, as you can learn, that in shaping a story you can do your conscious best with it and then lay it aside for a while, and return to it later to discover that, unknown to you, your subconscious mind has been busy working out many of the details and filling in the plan.

Having searched yourself, having explored and *agitated* your hidden potential, and having come into rapport, as it were, with that marvelous record of all that you are, you will be well on your way to the creative act. You will blunder and suffer and despair, for there is no guide, no formula, no rules. You will learn by writing. Though your first efforts may be of small worth, Pliny the Elder, as reported by his nephew, said that no book is so bad but that some good may be got out of it. You will at least get the good of practice. You can comfort yourself with the fact that nearly all established writers today wrote a lot of shoddy stuff which they published to their shame or manfully destroyed. My first published novel was my sixth, and I am glad that publishers rejected the first five, which I destroyed long ago. Indeed most of us could be glad if some of our published things had been rejected.

You will need great courage, and moral courage above all. The whole problem of artistic renunciation, says Rank, is "contained in the acceptance and knowledge that the creator must give a part of his life—in fact, his own life—

in order to make it eternal in his work and art." Keep by you Mill's statement that there is "no philosophy possible where fear of consequences is a stronger principle than love of truth." You will stick to it if the will in you to create is strong. You will look round you and observe with Holmes's Autocrat that "nothing strikes one more than to see how many give out in the first half of the course"—or in the first quarter. If you wish to know how many have given out in the last three decades go back through the literary journals and discover the number of authors of promising first novels, or even of two or three, who have vanished from the scene, or have become the hired hacks of the popular journals. Among them were some with great talent; but in this most commercial of nations, where art like steel can be established in public esteem only by a safe six per cent, talent is not enough. You will have to root, hog, or die.

Among these general remarks, which it is hoped may give you some clue to your resources, the concluding word will be about your reading habits. The man of imagination without learning, said Joubert, has wings but no feet. Very few of the great writers, says Maxwell Perkins in his "Letters," had formal education and many of them "never mastered spelling or grammar." He thought that the way "they teach literature and writing in colleges is harmful. It results in one getting into the habit of seeing everything through a kind of film of past literature." That may be so; but a writer, I think, needs feet as well as wings, because knowledge has become so specialized and departmentalized that sometimes the persons in the same profession or field can understand one another only at the most general points of contact. The task of the writer is synthesis and all knowledge must continue to be his province. Yet it must be said that among writers are some of the most ill-informed and ill-educated persons on earth. They may mistake, as Dos Passos has said, perspiration for inspiration, but more probably they have the notion that inspiration is an adequate substitute for knowledge.

I have before me the statement of an American novelist who, on being asked to name his favorite book, said of the Old Testament: "Whatever special knowledge anyone has discovered in any field, one finds corroborated in it. It has intuitive anticipation of everything that happens."[6] The

---

[6] *Look*, June 7, 1949.

statement is so fantastically silly that one wonders whether this man is living in the twentieth century or in the tenth. He calls to mind Goethe's well-known observation that few people "know what time and trouble it costs to *learn* to read." He had been working at it eighteen years, said Goethe, and was not yet successful. He calls to mind an observation by Arnold, that one must be struck "more and more the longer one lives, to find how much in our present society a man's life of each day depends for its solidity and value upon whether he reads during that day, and far more still on what he reads during it." He calls to mind a statement by Delacroix: "A human mind abandoned to itself always falls back into stupid childhood."

I would not say that any writer ought to read as much as I have read but I do think that most young writers do not read enough of the right thing and far too much of the wrong thing. I have observed in them a tendency to confine their reading largely to the work of their colleagues. There is no reason why we should not read the contemporaries in our field, and particularly our superiors; but we can not afford to forget the words of Santayana, that those who can not remember the past are condemned to repeat it. Knowledge of the past no less than of the present, and possibly even more, certainly ought to be a part of any creator's equipment. Indeed, knowledge of the present is impossible without knowledge of the past: no enlightened person in these times tries to understand the adult without going back to the child, nor the child without going back into his heritage. Think how different the world might be at this moment (spring, 1952) if F. D. Roosevelt had read and *understood* Machiavelli, Lenin and Stalin!

It is not only that the past throws its shadow upon the present. It *is* the present. There exists, said the great author of the *Golden Bough*, "such a solid layer of savagery beneath the surface of society, unaffected by the superficial changes of religion and culture" that the "dispassionate observer, whose studies have led him to plumb its depths, can hardly regard it otherwise than as a standing menace to civilization." With what thoroughness the world supported those words after his death! Do you understand what he meant? These survivals from a primitive age are everywhere you look—in mourning garments and color, in the tolling of bells, heraldic crests, mascots and badges, staff and spire and mistletoe, mother-in-law jokes, the kiss-

ing of the bride (B. K's daughter understood *that* one),
fast days and rest days, charivari, plum puddings and bon-
fires and hot-cross buns, the cross, the vestments of the
clergy, church architecture, Easter, Christmas, Sunday—
there is no end of them, and we are all of us (with some
of them willingly) their prisoners. Frazer had in mind of
course the emotions rather than the symbols, but the symbols
perpetuate and nourish the emotions.

It may not be assumed that most so-called literate persons
are aware of all this. We certainly dare not imagine that
the novelist was, for whom the Old Testament anticipates
all knowledge; or a book critic who wrote me that I erred
in supposing that primitive people felt actual blood kinship
with beasts; or another who wrote me to deny indignantly
that the early Christians assimilated Mary to Isis. The
shofar or rams-horn was used anciently by Jews to frighten
evil spirits away; yet when, during the last great war, I
published a statement to that effect, several Jewish officers
at a near-by air base sent me angry letters that accused me
of gross and malicious ignorance.

On the basis of my experience, which includes nine years
as a teacher in American universities, I would say that
ignorance of the past in all but a fraction of the people
can not possibly be exaggerated. When I asked a nationally
known educator what he thought might be the psychology
of the fact that ancient peoples ate their gods he looked
at me blankly and said, "I didn't know they did." Has
he never thought at all about the doctrine of transub-
stantiation? When I asked an eminent psychologist if
in assimilating Jesus to the pagan savior-god the Christians
were elaborating on the scapegoat idea he said he had never
heard of either. And another eminent psychologist, a friend
of mine, has solemnly told me that knowledge of the past
is of no importance at all.

I'm not advising you to become a pale and cloistered
person hidden away in libraries. Keep before you, if you
will, Borrow's apple-woman in *Lavengro:* "So here was a
woman who attributed the vices and follies of her life to
being able to read; her mother, she said, who could not read,
lived respectably and died in peace."

But without vision there is no art, and it takes the works
of a lot of minds to nourish a vision. J. M. Robertson somewhere speaks of that "unfruitful conservatism to which our
mental laziness is so prone." Writers can not afford the

he would rather die than not keep up the pose are we to be so cruel as to say that suicide was only an effort to preserve the ego within the self-protective assumptions? Or shall we say with Barzun that what the preposterous child needs is some damned good discipline?

Now such writers as Lawrence, Kafka and Proust, to name only three, were such spoiled children that no protective pose was able to hide their real souls. They were visible even to obtuse observers. In a book before me it is said that when Proust was invited out to dinner he always ate before he went because he preferred his own talk to any food that could be set before him. Not so long ago I sat in a group when a young novelist was angry and bitter in his denunciation of Katherine Anne Porter. He was denouncing her poses, possibly because he preferred his own. One reason that authors don't like to meet one another is that their harsh opinions of one another are usually so shameful. And everywhere their votaries are busy trying to justify and exalt their outrageous behavior. How was it with the more saintly figures, such as Charles Dickens? Monica Dickens has written of him that he "was selfish and demanding. . . . He could be moody and unreliable, but the man was a genius, don't forget." Ah, there we have it! The mythmakers have built up the revered and practically unassailable notion that "genius" is different, and never to be judged by the standards of twelve good men and true. It lives in another world, we are told, and is to be judged by laws of its own contriving; and if anyone questions these laws he is to be dismissed as an illiterate ingrate who would do well to stick to what he can understand.

The notion may have a little truth in it but in this sentimental and "romantic" country it has been carried far into the realm of nonsense. If the apotheosized Dickens was a selfish tyrant dare lesser men point the fact out? Shall we not leave him enshrined in the textbooks for school kids? George Meredith complained constantly of neglect, which did not in fact exist; and though I spent a year of research and a doctoral thesis exploding the myth of his neglect, it still endures and is still taught in our universities. If Thomas Mann, now vanishing into myth, and becoming a symbol along with the Baruchs of semidivine wisdom, can say, as indeed he has, and in the ripeness of his old age at that, that art can develop as fully under a tyranny, such as the Russian, as in a country that allows much more freedom to creative talent, are we to be astonished by those who vanish into Mexico or jump off ships into the sea? Leuba has said that the early Christians tried to make an idea the reality. Does it follow that if an artist cannot make his ideas the realities for the world he is justified in suicide or in a loud and triumphant return to a moribund church or in disappearing into the abracadabra of his subconscious mind? Or shall we say that there is a danger in the lack of self-discipline in those who have so much influence on the course of human events? Bearing in mind that all this is the stuff of myth and legend, dare we ask what part was played by the pathetically adolescent "lost generation" school of writers in making the world vulnerable to a second great war?

"Man," wrote Lippert, the eminent sociologist, "regarding himself as the center of things, is inclined at all times to regard the advantageous and the pleasurable as the normal and expected course of things, and the unpleasant as a disturbance and interruption of it." When, years ago, I tried to teach the writing of the short-story or novel I sometimes said to my students: "Before me are twenty intelligent persons who want to be writers; yet every one of you regards himself as the exact center of the universe, with its limits equidistant from you at all points; and when you move you carry the center of the universe around with you." They admitted that so it seemed to be. And I told them of a renowned professor of astronomy under whom I had once sat who solemnly said to his students that if there exists in other parts of the universe what we call life it is inferior to the life on our dinky little planet. Self-protective assumptions can hardly go farther than that. A news magazine[1] commenting on the theory of a German astronomer said that according to his notion "many millions of similar stars may have planets. If so, there is a chance that higher forms of life, perhaps higher than man, may have developed on some of them." Only a chance among millions, mind you; and *perhaps* the forms in some instances have been higher than the ridiculous apes you see all around you, who at the present moment are frantically getting ready for a third vast slaughter in one generation. It seems to occur to none of these egoists that if the universe has always been here—and no other assumption is conceivable —life quite certainly has developed in countless times and

---

[1] *Time*, Oct. 24, 1949.

places. Or if that is not true, we must face the shocking alternative that we are anomalous. A year later, *Time* was considering another theory of the universe, that of Hoyle and Lyttleton, and concluded that if they are correct, the universe "has no beginning and no end, no middle and no circumference in either time or space. It is hard to start describing such an endless, beginningless object." It is indeed, for us simians, with our dull little minds that have taken so much for granted.

No ridicule, said Meredith, knocks the strength out of us so thoroughly as our own; but with all the cunning we have we dodge it, or even candid criticism, and none more than the artists. There is nothing in the world that is certain, said Pliny, save that nothing is certain, and "there is no more wretched and yet arrogant being than man." Somewhere in his *Diaries* Tschaikovsky says of Tolstoy that "he liked to disavow Beethoven and frankly expressed doubts about his genius." Then he adds this luminous comment: "This trait is not at all characteristic of great people; to reduce to one's own *incomprehension* a genius acknowledged by all is a characteristic of *limited people.*" We are all severely limited people, so far as that goes.

In dealing with artists we are dealing with children. We are dealing with abnormally vain, egocentric, envious, unhappy people. The symptom, says an axiom in psychology, is the patient's friend. We are dealing with people who so cherish and nourish their symptoms and abnormal traits, including their vices, that of those who go to psychiatrists none seems to return changed.

Take, for instance, a poet and two novelists who once sat in my home drinking cocktails and talking. The two novelists and I, warmed by liquor and fellowship, said a great deal and said it poorly. After it was all over, the poet, who had not uttered a word, sought me out and exploded: "You Goddamned neurotics are enough to make a good psychotic p—— his pants!"

There you have it said superlatively well. This poet is convinced that he is a schizoid and he rides his horse pretty hard. The schizoid, let us remember, is the aristocrat among the "abnormals." And how jealously they all cling to their distinction! This man is a poet with a fine mind and a fine talent; but more than that, you see, he has something precious that sets him apart from commonplace neurotics, whom he abhors. Most of us are only neurotics. A psychotic,

God bless him, is a prince among us, with his deeper consciousness, his fascinating ambivalence, and a surer path
to the sources of mysticism and poetry. With luck he can
hope to go insane, whereas most of us, with our compulsions
and obsessions and tics and phobias, will endure to our
death in that borderland between the sane and the insane,
picking up arthritis, neuritis, ulcers, constipation and the
various other crippling but never fatal ailments which
neurotics enjoy in common.

A fine study in the neurotic temperament is to be found in
Flaubert's letters to a friend, to whom he complained end-
lessly while writing a book, saying that "I grow so hard to
please as a literary artist that I am driven to despair. I
shall end by not writing another line." Various academic
critics have approached his letters with awe, entirely
missing the self-pitying martydom and the childish mythmaking, and concluding that here was the artist's artist,
the man who almost went mad (he himself said so) trying
to find the unique word for his unique meaning. In regard
to this interesting pose the chapter on Words will have
something to say.

Was the schizoid poet sincere? Did Thomas Wolfe have,
as Mr. Muller believes, passionate sincerity in all his work?
The answer to both questions is yes and no: they both
thought they were sincere but under their pose was a deep,
dark and depressing insincerity. They call to mind one of
Black's characters who said that most dangerous of all "was
a gift of sincerity that deceived himself. He could assume
an opinion or express an emotion at will, with such genuine
fervor that he himself forgot how recently he had acquired
it." That is the curse of all the Hamlets. In the mythology
of the subject it is widely believed that of all persons on
earth, artists are the most sincere, second only to theologians. But let us be done with this silly myth. Sincerity
like everything else is relative. Complete sincerity could
be possible only in one who fully understood his motives
and the motives in human nature. Such a person has not
yet lived among us and we dare not suppose that he ever will.

We are dealing here in depths of consciousness; or, to
put it another way, we are dealing with the various degrees
in which the subconscious permeates and enriches the
conscious mind. We are dealing—to use two words which a
certain school of psychologists is trying to abandon without
offering adequate substitutes—with the extrovert and the

introvert. These words mean different things to different people. As I use them in this book they mean only, or at least chiefly, a difference in depth of consciousness, extreme extroversion being very shallow in its emotional and mental processes, that is, largely surfaced; and introversion ranging all the way from morbid shyness to the depth found in such a writer as Lawrence, and from there to that almost intimate union of the conscious and subconscious minds in which the schizoid mystic lives.

Subtlety in insincerity depends of course on depth of consciousness. Simple extroverted people do not fool us, even when they try to—and they are everlastingly trying to. Their evasions are too clumsy, their mental processes are too shallow. Those with deeper consciousness can fool us, and worse than that they can fool themselves. This practice of deception, usually undeliberate, and in the deceiver himself usually unperceived, occupies the proportions of a disease among artists everywhere and among their cultists. Very few of us struggle successfully, as Wells believed he was able to, against self-protective devices. It was easier for Tolstoy to disparage a fellow artist than to drag forth his buried motives and look at them. It was easier for the novelist to denounce Miss Porter than to look into his own depths. It was easier for the poet to denounce neurotics than to face the reasons why he is psychotic. And it is always easy to encourage friends, readers and critics to insulate us with the self-protective myths.

We will now look at a few forms which this insulation takes.

A common delusion with authors (I have heard it voiced a number of times) is the notion that when they write they become another and "higher" person. George Eliot said that in the production of all her best work there was another, a "not herself," who took possession of her; that she became "merely the instrument through which the spirit acted." Other authors have left in journals or letters similar confessions, all of which are meaningless unless we suppose that in periods of intense concentration the subconscious mind to a large extent takes over. I cannot say that this is so. The most I can honestly confess to is this, that when deeply immersed in my work I am sometimes unaware of the sounds around me, including, my wife tells me, the sound of my name. But if this is so there is nothing mysterious about it. Such concentration most people can

come to with effort and practice. The idea that another
person or spirit takes over goes back to ancient superstition. Even an author of the stature of Goethe said that
when emotionally aroused he felt psychic pain, which he
had to relieve by writing. I haven't a ghost of a notion of
what he meant by psychic pain.

R. Henning in a study of inspiration some decades back
polled more than fifty writers. George Sand said that she
was "another person" when she wrote; Mrs. Stowe, that
she did not know that Uncle Tom was dead until she read
about it; Hardy, that he was sometimes practically unconscious when composing. Some said they suffered seizures,
and so were unable to explain how they actually got their
work done. We must regard all such confessions with
cynical incredulity, for they are products of the child
mind: it is a commonplace observation that children have
no power to distinguish between the false and the true.
Goethe said that "all productivity of the highest kind,
every important conception, every discovery, every great
thought which bears fruit, is in no one's control, and is
beyond every earthly power. Such things are to be regarded
as unexpected gifts from above, as pure divine products."
That such silliness could come from so great a writer sug-
gests that a hard look at the mythmakers is no waste of our
time.

And then there are those authors, usually of a lower
order of achievement, who contend that they have to have
a strange self-induced atmosphere before they can create.
They must eat onions or sit with their feet in a hot bath
or breathe the scent of musk or have a mandrake poultice
on their brow or a cud of fenugreek under their tongue or
a photograph of the well-beloved on the desk. Such vagaries
are as common as the tics and twitches in the anxiety
neurotic. When I lived in New York City I went now and
then to a Village underground lair to contemplate a minor
poet who, while composing, sat on the floor, drinking tea
through a stem twenty feet long, while the madame softly
tiptoed around to tell us not to disturb the great man. It
is a sufficient comment on such "creators" to say that their
stuff is never accepted by any but the few members of their
cult, and by those only until they can discover a fresh god.

And there is the common and childlike belief in inspiration. When Dos Passos said that some writers mistake
perspiration for inspiration I cannot imagine what he meant

or believe that he meant anything at all. Belief in inspiration, like that in possession, ghosts and psychic pain, goes back to the childhood of the race. If one believes in inspiration one must also believe in guidance by a higher power that uses one as an instrument. That was all right in the time of Paul but it is no good today. Nobody is inspired. If you must think that you are then by all means cherish the illusion, but accept it as you accept a rabbit's-foot, the horseshoe above the door, the mascot and badge, or any other fetish of ancient times. If you are so dubious of your talent that you must clothe it with the follies of primitive peoples it might be well to take a good look at yourself in a mirror.

We are gravely assured by one of his editors that Flaubert had on his tongue for days the flavor of the poison with which Madame Bovary killed herself. That is possible if he was a hysteric and had a certain poison in mind and tasted it. It is more likely that the mythmaker has been busy. A great number of similar things have been said about various people of the past and are being said about some of those of the present. It is not so much a question whether you will become a victim of the mythmakers as whether you will be fool enough to encourage them. In regard to that let us for a moment consider the case of Thomas Wolfe, who was being engulfed by myth even before he died at the age of thirty-eight.

He was, of course, the kind of man who is born and built for the mythmakers. Too huge for ordinary beds or clothes or automobiles, too tall for ordinary windows and doors, he came upon the American scene with a book to match his size; and Americans, with their infantile interest in bigness of all kinds, including altitudes and olives, took him to their hearts. Wolfe's appetites like his frame were big but they were never so big as he imagined them to be, and I speak as one who knew him well.[2] With the publication of his first book the myth started and he pitched in to help it grow. One of the themes running through his volumes is *devouring*. At once the Wolfe protagonist, who is always Wolfe himself, began to devour everything in sight—books, food, drink, women, far places, and everything else that a titan could possibly feed on. Everything from then on was oversized, and from wonder to wonder the size grew. Little men gazed upon him with astonishment. Little women

[2] See for instance my articles on Wolfe in *Tomorrow*, April and July, 1951.

placed themselves in the way of easy capture. And he began
to take everything as his right. He was becoming a legend,
and to fertilize the legend he made his manuscripts bigger
and bigger; and the mythmakers got busy with these also,
spreading the story that they were delivered in bales by
truck. He tried to become the symbol of what he thought
his country's meaning was. I sat with him one morning at
breakfast and he devoured enough for ten men. He wolfed
it down, to use another of his favorite words; but closely
observing him I was not at all persuaded that he was
conscious of eating. He was simply taken over body and
soul by the job of being big—big in his eating, his love-
making, his journeying, his talk, his dreams and ambitions
and books; and so he easily came by the notion, as Maxwell
Perkins has said, that a good book had to be big in physical
size.

That is all right but for the fact that Wolfe was being
defeated by the myth. If Wolfe had lived it would have
been fascinating to watch the labors of the mythmakers as
the myth developed. The myth was engulfing him, and in
trying to fill its stupendous vacuum he was losing sight of
the man. He was in grave danger of losing sight of life
itself and going off into the stratosphere like a wandering
nebula. The mythmakers—and never forget this, for this
is one of the few important things this book has to tell you
—the mythmakers eat what they build, as in times past
they ate their gods. The thing created is at last destroyed
by its over-zealous creators. In ancient times people ate
their gods, and later their god-surrogates, such as the bull
and lamb; and today they create their gods only to devour
them. They project into them their buried fantasies, absorb
and assimilate them, cast off the waste product and proceed
to the next meal. It takes an artist of tough fiber to develop
in his votaries a case of indigestion. I should imagine that
Mr. Cabell has been cellulose in more alimentary canals
than that of Mr. Granville Hicks, but that Mr. Hemingway,
to whom we shall come in a moment, has become another
sacrificial lamb. George Bernard Shaw, who became such
willing fodder to the god-eaters, could have given some
pertinent remarks here, for at the time of his death he was
little more than an eructed phantom. Keep in mind that
Church dogma which, as Henry Osborn Taylor puts it,
"embraced the spiritual realism of Augustine, according to
which the ultra reality of the Eucharistic elements consisted

in the *virtus sacramenti*, that is, in their miraculous and
real, but invisible, transformation into the veritable substance of Christ's veritable body." The "misbeliever . . .
ate not Christ's body, but his own *judicium*, his own deeper
damnation." As far back as records go people have been
trying to absorb the qualities in their heroes which they
admire and covet. The symbolic process today is subtler
than in ancient times, and for that reason all the more
difficult to be aware of. If you do not choose to be eaten,
digested and absorbed into the common legendary heritage
of the folk-mind you must develop art for the sophisticated
palate. You will, of course, be assimilated eventually, with
only your name left to mark the spot.

Here are instances of the way the mythmakers, that is,
the god-creators, work. In the *New Yorker* profile of Rex
Stout, Alva Johnston wrote, in building up his hero, that
Stout's father "had an extraordinary library. It consisted
of about twelve hundred volumes of biography, history,
fiction, philosophy, science and poetry. Rex had read them
all by the time he was eleven." John McNulty protested
the absurdity, and Johnston replied by piling myth on
myth, exhumed from the shades of the past. He dragged
forth the ghost of John Stuart Mill, who "started writing
histories at six and a half; Macaulay, who had read enough
to do a universal history at nine"; as well as Crichton,
Van Anda, and Clifton Fadiman whose "camera-eye" can,
we are told, photostat a whole page in a "very few seconds."
A few months later *Time,* equally solemn and credulous,
wrote of Sir Oliver Franks that he "raced through most
of the weighty philosophical tomes in his father's vast
library by the time he was twelve." A *vast* library is quite
a library. Franks seemed to have the edge on Stout until
a disgusted reader wrote in: "Just say he had read as
widely as any precocious twelve-year-old." Which is still
a lot to settle for. Helen Waddell tells of Alexander Neckam
and Eberhard the German who, in drawing up courses in
the arts, "perhaps a little exaggerated their reading: it is
the eternal temptation of bibliographers"—and of mythologists, as you perceive.

Another author who has been set apart for apotheosis is
Mr. Hemingway, and his chief mythologists seem to be
Malcolm Cowley and John O'Hara, with minor ones active
farther out. The attitude of both Cowley and O'Hara
toward this writer is something for the book—or should

I say for the psychologist? Take, for instance, an essay in *Life* in which Cowley gravely set down as truth such matters as these: that Hemingway's sons "worship" their father; that Hemingway does not smoke because he chooses to preserve "his keen sense of smell"; that he has scars from his crown to his feet and was "always getting injured"; that he is "romantic by nature and falls in love like a big hemlock crashing down through the underbrush"; and then this startling observation, that before commencing to write in the morning "he reads what he has written already— the whole novel, until he is halfway through writing it, and two or three chapters in any case." Now if an author does a novel of a hundred thousand words and reads through the first half of it each morning while composing the last half, and composes an average of five hundred words a day, by the time the book is completed he will have read the first half a hundred times! Well, Evelyn Waugh has been quoted as saying that he read his novel *Helena* a score of times after it was published. If these things are true of Waugh and Hemingway we can only stand aghast at the indulgence they feel for their own stuff.

In *Collier's* (Nov. 18, 1950) there appeared an editorial, with a colorful drawing above it by Al Hirschfeld, in which Hemingway, represented as a hairy and triumphant colossus, stands with his left foot on a prostrate Shakespeare, his left hand grasping his dripping spear, while around him in postures of grotesque defeat are a score of the greatest writers of the past three hundred years. The editorial gives the first paragraph of O'Hara's New York *Times* front-page review (Sept. 10, 1950) of *Across the River and into the Trees:* "The most important author living today, the outstanding author since the death of Shakespeare. . . . The author, of course, is Ernest Hemingway, the most important, the outstanding author of the millions of writers who have lived since 1616." The editorial writer says that he reread the review "carefully several times under a strong light. It was our implausible hope that we might have misread it before, but it always came out the same." In fairness to Hemingway it should be pointed out that in placing himself above writers since Shakespeare he made an exception of Tolstoy. Mr. O'Hara apparently thought that an unnecessary piece of indulgence on Hemingway's part.

One would like to dismiss the whole thing as a big hoax. But Mr. Evelyn Waugh, whose incredible fondness for his

below that level, as artists too commonly do who are betrayed by those who would glorify them.

A recent instance of mythmaking at its worst appeared in the *Reader's Digest* (March, 1950) where Herbert Corey solemnly attributes to Willmot Lewis the old witticism, "I felt like a lion in a den of Daniels," gravely adding that since Lewis said it in 1931 this bon mot has enlivened the orations of hundreds of speakers. A roomful of us (I think John Gunther was present) heard Professor James Weber Linn try to pass it off as his own in 1922 or 1923. A source before me says it is much older than that.

We now come to one of the important things this book has to tell you. Unless you are sure that your mind can perceive the motives and your vanity resist the blandishments flee from your idolaters as you would from bedlam. Unless you wish to exploit the credulity, superstitions, ignorance and hero-worshiping tendencies in people, and at last get hung up in a web, abjure the mythmakers. Abjure the efforts of the god-abandoned or god-seeking to bring you to the apotheosis, for they have no interest in the gods they create but only in the reflection of their image in their creations. The life of an artist has enough hazards without being put in the way of a god-creating and god-eating mankind. For in ancient times—let me repeat it—people ate their gods, and in ways subtly and wondrously refined they still destroy them.

ART *vs.* MERCHANDISE

"Every man's work shall be made manifest: for
the day shall declare it, because it shall be revealed
by fire; and the fire shall try every man's work of
what sort it is."—I CORINTHIANS

I DO NOT have, though, alas, I formerly did have, that
contempt which is so common in artists for those who are
ordinarily dismissed as journalists and hacks. These serve
a purpose, particularly in a democracy; and it may be that
there they serve a greater purpose than the artist serves.
I have heard thoughtful persons express such an opinion.
Life, they say, is for the great majority dull and empty
enough. One must agree with that. It is in fact a riddle to
me, who have read so much about the ancient world, how
people then, with so much less to interest and comfort them
than we have now, got along at all without going insane.
Possibly it was because, as Professor Case puts it, the sky
hung low in the ancient world. Imagination was confined,
communication was difficult, travel was severely limited,
and ignorance was king.

A great many people today live vicariously, and such
institutions as Hollywood, such mediums as popular magazines, not only with their fiction but even more with their
advertising, offer the stuff that common emotions feed on.
To measure this phenomenon, so peculiar to the modern
world, you have only to observe the number of columns
which newspapers give, not alone to murder and rape and
other kinds of crime and violence, but to the trivial doings
of the popular heroes. Insanity is increasing; our asylums
are overfilled. The diseases inherent in the "civilized" life
still march some leagues ahead of our medical skills. In
spite of their high standard of material living, their com-
forts, their myths and their political messiahs we have a
neurotic and unhappy people. It would therefore be poor
grace in me or in you or in anyone to deny to the masses
that vicarious nourishment which, even if it does not pro-

mote their sanity or instruct them in the difficult task of living fully and wisely, does nevertheless help them along in life, filling their souls with shoddy wonders as they go.

But for all that we must recognize that there is art— though quite what art is I don't pretend to know; and there is that huge body of popular fiction which seems to have become as necessary to the emotionally illiterate people as their deodorants and Diors. In this chapter we are going to consider the two groups, the artists, and those who frankly write for money and a large and essentially un-educated audience.

We may as well realize at once that the two groups overlap, that some who affect to be artists are only doubt-fully so, that some in the popular group stoutly maintain that they are artists, and may be. Sometimes the cleavage between the two is animated by bitterness and spleen. I had this truth pressed upon me many years ago when I sat one evening in a Spokane home with four other writers. Three of them were among the most successful pulp writers in the Northwest. One of these three was a woman. Two of the men were tall, broad, handsome fellows, quite illiterate, extroverted, wholesome, aggressive, unabashed. The four of them talked and I listened; and since they were talking about their own work, as writers invariably do if given a chance, and since they were aware that present among them was a queer creature who possibly held Street and Smith writers in contempt, they directed their remarks at me. It was they who felt contempt for me. They mistook my morbid shyness for arrogance.

"These writers," said one of the fullbacks, whom we'll call Jim, "who think they're artists, good Jesus, they give me a gutache. Writing is writing, I tell you. Some of us make money, the others don't, and they starve in their garrets and crap about art. They make my old gut ache!" he cried and looked at me.

"I make twenty thousand a year," said John. "Twenty grand, by God. How many of these damned art scribblers make that much?"

"Well," said Jim, "I'll tell you. I've tried to read these so-called artists but they stick in my plenum. Take this guy Faulkner—who in hell reads him? His wife? By God, how could any normal person read that guff? Silly crap about a guy who fell in love with a horse!"

"I think it was a goat," said Mary. "The trouble with

these people," she went on, her malice making a glowing thing of her face, "is that they can't get in the *Post* and the other big money. They're just envious, that's all."

"Envious as hell," said John.

"Hell's do-hickey," said Jim, "they're worse than that. They're morbid, by God, that's their trouble. Look at all these little magazines they print their crap in. They don't get paid a thin dime for it. And who in hell reads it? Their wives?"

"Not their wives," said Mary. "Their mothers maybe."

"Why write if nobody pays you for it and nobody reads you?" He looked hard at me. "Fisher, what's your answer?"

"I—" I said, turning pink. "Well—"

"Well what?" asked John.

"Who reads your stuff?" asked Jim. "All that morbid crap about a kid named Vridar. How much did that book make you?"

"About four hundred," I said.

"God's do-hickey! How long did it take you to write it?"

"Oh, about two years."

"Holy Caesar! Two hundred bucks a year!"

And so it went during a long evening.

A few times, also many years ago, I sat with a group of artists, or with persons anyway who would have been mortally offended if you had called them by any other name—poets, painters, art critics. I thought them even more absurd. Artists, as I have known them, are even more intolerant and scornful than the extroverts trying to dope out the *Post* "angle." Art—art—art is the word forever on their tongue—a totem, a fetish, a cult. Such people nourish their pose in exclusive little groups. In listening to those in Spokane I felt that the defect in them was no sense at all of their superiors. In listening to the artists in New York I felt that they were the prisoners of their cult.

Matisse has written: "There are always two kinds of painting. First there is the kind that introduces something new. Such paintings begin by being worthless but eventually they ascend the heights in value. Then there are those which are accepted at the outset because they offer nothing new but simply flatter the public taste. They are later found to be worthless."

It may be that Matisse was busy there making out a case for himself but there is some truth in what he says. Great art seldom appeals to the general public. But what *is* art?

Millions of words have been written about it but nobody has offered a definition that is widely accepted. Art, said Alfred Stevens, is "nature seen through the prism of an emotion." Art, said Wagner, is "an immediate vital act," adding that it is the expression of man, as man is the expression of nature. Art, said Hebbel, is "the conscience of mankind"; and again: "In art, as in everything living, there is no progress but only varieties of one stimulus." Art, said Galsworthy, is that "which warms one with unconscious vibration." Art, said Strzygowski, "translates inward meaning into visible form; it uses the creative skill of man to free it from the limitations of life." Art, says my dictionary, "is the application of skill and taste to production according to aesthetic principles." Aesthetics, it says, is "the science of the beautiful." Now obviously all such definitions are mere impressionistic flashes. I have a friend who talks about art incessantly and when I ask her what she means by art she says icily: "If at your age you don't know what art is you'll never know." I have no doubt of that, but in this book I must use the word, just as I must use the word soul without knowing what it means to anyone.

I would think that in its broadest sense we mean by art the arrangement of materials for the greatest illumination of their substance. But the greatest illumination for whom? Cabell and Faulkner, fine artists at their summits, have never been and could never be popular in their own generation. Hemingway, on the other hand, regarded by some as an excellent artist, has a huge popular audience. Plainly enough his art form is far less subtle than that of the other two. There is also, of course, the matter of substance. Cabell's substance, his themes, even when lifted out of their art-form and expressed in simple words, are intelligible only to people who have done a great deal of reading and thinking. I learned as a teacher that some of those who dote on Hemingway cannot understand Cabell at all.

To make clear what I mean I must digress.

When I taught a course in the contemporary novel I included *The Silver Stallion, Something About Eve* and *A Farewell to Arms*. Sitting before me in New York were forty or fifty students, most of them Jews, most of them considerably above the national average (as I found it anyway) for juniors and seniors. Hemingway's book they grasped without any trouble at all, and liked it; but in three years of teaching there I had no more than three or four students who were able to grasp the truths in the Cabell books, even after I had done my best to explain them. More than that, among all my friends I know of none who likes Cabell. It is not so much his art-form which repels them; the truths in his book outrage their self-esteem. They are truths that we can grasp only if we see in a mirror more than the countenance of the well-beloved.

And now, to return. "I perceive," said Lothair, "that life is not so simple an affair as I had once supposed." For the popular writer it is a very simple affair. He so oversimplifies it that he strips it down to a few commonplace precepts, perceptions and formulas. His point of view is essentially that of the "romantic." And at this point another digression is called for.

I once gave a talk to some of the graduate students and faculty in a large university. My subject was "Romance and Realism." When I had concluded, a faculty member, then unknown to me, but later identified as a psychiatrist, blurted: "You remind me of nothing so much as the pathological rantings of some of my patients!" That was abrupt and ungracious but it was plain. A year later I gave the same talk to a federation of women's clubs. A number of persons walked out while I was speaking, and when I had concluded the audience was openly hostile. What had I said to offend these people? Only these things—and after fifteen years I see no compelling reason to abandon them: that Meredith was right when he said that a frank acceptance of reality is the only firm basis of the ideal; that the huge American complex of vague and tenuous meanings (or emotions) called romance has been largely born of a refusal to accept reality frankly for what it is; that "romance" is essentially the escape mechanism of an extroverted, neurotic, sentimental and emotionally immature people; and that the realist is trying to strip away the useless myths, legends, cult-fantasies and all the other self-protective devices. I have long believed that Cabell is the greatest realist who has yet written in this country—that by comparison with him, Lewis, Wolfe and Steinbeck, to name only three, are romantics of the first water. I said in my talk that for me Cabell is not a romantic at all. That his fellow-countrymen have dismissed him as a romantic—and by such as Granville Hicks as a "venal" romantic at that—can mean only that their self-protective assumptions do not allow them to understand him. To discover with what delightfully urbane

over us was a great and compassionate Father who marked
the fall of every feather and the sprouting of every seed.
All that is now no more. But the search for higher truths
will go on, and those insulated with self-protective assumptions who cannot endure the ordeal will have the results of
their revolt buried with their bones. We have found no
answer to Job's question. We have not been able to add a
single word of wisdom to the bitter philosophy of the
Preacher. Lost, O lost! was Wolfe's favorite cry and his
own title for his first novel; and his cry seemed to find a
response in the hearts of his countrymen. As science has
destroyed the foundations created by the primitive folk-
mind people have indeed been feeling that they are lost,
that their towers beyond tragedy have crumbled, that faith
itself may disappear. The greatest change in the history of
mankind, a scholar has said, was that from the natural to
the supernatural world. Two thousand years ago, for all
but a few, the supernatural was practically the only world,
miracles were commonplace, and the ascent of heroes to
heaven on their death was accepted as an ordinary fact.
But today we are abandoning the concept of the supernatural and the time must come when there will be nothing
left of it. God has again become remote, inapprehensible,
lost. From the Persians the Jews took the idea of angels
and used them to restore the divine intimacy. The early
Christians brought God down in the Logos-Christ. Today
a spiritually undernourished people, having again lost God
in the depths of the universe, are returning, as these pages
said earlier, to emperor-worship, with its religion of the
State. Or they are trying to whistle in the dark with what
in this country goes under the name of romance.

We can have no objection to that. People must do what
they feel impelled to do in their efforts to keep their sanity.
We are, it seems to me, in a great period of transition, between those two worlds of Matthew Arnold, one dead, the
other striving to be born; and until we can again find the
earth under our feet, firm and warm and friendly, we shall
have to stand on old or new myths with such fortitude as
we can manage. But our bewilderment and loss are no
reason to confuse the issue. It brings us nothing to say, as
a critic has recently said, that Faulkner is "one of the great
romantic writers of our time." As I understand him he is
nothing of the sort. He is employing the techniques of the
schizoid personality (society itself has become schizoid),

of the subconscious, and of the southern myth. Nor is it true as I see it that his concern is primarily with the disintegration of the South. That disintegration is only a small part of worldwide crumbling of faiths and dogmas.

I am trying to suggest that the serious artist today faces problems vastly more complex than those of his predecessors. Life is not the simple affair that it was for Dante, Milton, Dickens and Balzac. And because it has become a very complex affair many persons choose those modes of behavior which make the least exhausting demands on their emotions. A popular novelist, Lloyd Douglas, expressed this view when he said that he is "staunchly opposed to change" and that changelessness is his only theme because people "long to stay put." But truth, as the ancient Greeks perceived, is a panorama of continuous change. Today the unalterable dogma has no secure place in it. Douglas is doubtless right in thinking that most people prefer the changeless; their emotions are more comfortable in it, as their bodies are in old clothes or their opinions among old friends. This is why truth has always been an alien or an outcast for all but the most intelligent and adventurous spirits, who, by frank acceptance of the realities and by rigorous self-discipline, adapt themselves to the demands on their emotions and minds.

"Dark seriousness and melancholy," said Lippert, "are the result of an accumulation of foresight." The artist today feels pretty dark and serious and sad. He may exclaim with Thomas Deloney, "Life, why, what is it but a floure, a bubble in the water, a spanne long and full of misery!" Well, in art it can be a little more than that. Art cannot define the meaning of meaning but it can give to meanings a slight permanence, so that we can grasp them for support while climbing Flammonde's hill.

There is yet another matter here for the young writer to consider. The poet who burst forth against neurotics sent me a group of questions, among them this: "What is the particular thing, if there is any, that differentiates man from the other animals?" I suppose it must be consciousness of self. Consciousness of self is the great blight on mankind today, and among us the schizoid should be able most fully to grasp that truth. Consciousness of self as a thing apart must surely have led, in the opinion of some who have written about it, to the concept of sin and the doctrine of atonement—of at-one-ment—at-one-ness. It was the individual, separated, and made conscious of his separateness, who strove to return to the group and the blessed nirvana of self-forgetfulness. The Prophets needed it but being unable to find it stood apart, aloof and solitary, thundering at the people about sin, depravity, and that at-one-ment which they themselves had no power to find. Aldous Huxley seems to have been trying to come to the at-one-ness: "The completely illuminated human being [as though there has been or could be one!] knows, with Law, that God 'is present in the deepest and most central part of his own soul' "— which may be what the medieval Hugo had in mind when he said, "The way to ascend to God is to descend into oneself." Is this nonsense? Boehme's disciple says to the master, "How may I attain supresensuous life, so that I may see God and hear him speak?" The master replies: "When you can lift yourself for one moment into that realm where no creature dwells you will hear what God speaks." "Is that near or far?" "It is in yourself." Calling attention to the fifth chapter of *De Signatura Rerum* Herbert Silberer says: "This theosophist makes such full use of the alchemistic symbolism, that we find it wherever we open his writings." Huxley reminds us that in the Indo-European languages the root meaning *two* connotes badness. It is to be wished that Huxley had proceeded in turn from the efforts of the ancients to make deity bisexual, to the split in the sexes, to the doctrine of at-onement. He speaks of the origin of good and evil, as though they had an origin, and he seems to accept the ancient and now foolish dualism of mind and matter.

Huxley says we can find God only by becoming godlike. No doubt. But do we become godlike with schizophrenic withdrawals into the depths of one's soul, or with empathy and projection? Does one contemplate one's navel or one's fellowmen? "I do not live," said Jose Ortega y Gasset. "I merely observe life." That may be one way to at-onement. It ought to be an easy way for artists, because most of them, indeed all those I have known, have gone bathing and got fused with the nymph. An eminent psychologist has expressed the belief that in human beings there is a subconscious effort to reunite the divided cell. The idea may seem fantastic, but even so, that may be what artists are trying to do. In any case, I wish that such fine minds as Huxley's, striving so valiantly to find the lantern in the dark, would dwell on that struggle toward at-onement which is today manifested in the tendency of the sexes to identify more and more with one another. It may be that such identification is necessary before they can find God. Even more, it may be that certain ancients looked to the deeper truth when they made God bisexual.

I am appealing here not to your emotions, which you use too much, but to your mind, which you use too little. I once read in a critic of some parts that the more mind an artist has the less artist he is likely to be. An elaboration of that matter could hardly omit Mr. Huxley, whose mind has always given the artist in him a great deal of trouble. Well, it may be that the artist doesn't need a critical and searching mind. Professor Wenley has said that the "mission of the great thinker usually proves to be twofold. He sums up the essential elements incident to the past and the present of the civilization he represents; and from the fresh height thus attained he issues direction for the future." But isn't that the function of the great artist? Or shall we accept the common opinion that he works with synthesis rather than with analysis, with intuitions rather than with thoughts?

I take the position that in this complex and difficult world the artist needs a good deal of mind if his work is to survive. Or shall we say more emotional maturity? For instance, one of the vices common of artists is their everlasting complaint about neglect. Meredith complained in a thousand letters, but only, so far as I was able to make out, because his royalty checks were so much smaller than those of Dickens and George Eliot. Professor Dill, writing of the time of Juvenal, speaks of "the complaints of the struggling man of letters about the extravagant rewards of low vulgar impostors." The rewards are still extravagant and artists still complain. Of Juvenal himself Dill says: "Conscious of great talents, with a character almost fierce in its energy, he felt a burning hatred of society which seemed to value only material success, or those supple and doubtful arts which could invent some fresh stimulus for exhausted appetites."

It sounds very modern and it is. In this most commercial of all nations, with its morbid deference to money and the social prominence which money begets, and with the big rewards in money and acclaim going to those who serve the vulgar, artists feel as Juvenal felt. Some of them express themselves with bitterness. Some of them, feeling bitterness toward the superficial culture of their own land, have taken up communism, because in Russia, they may tell you, as in New York they told me, the artist occupies a position worthy of his talent. But let nobody fool you. Any dictator in the world is glad to subsidize his ablest writers as propagandists, and the emoluments are exactly in proportion to the excellence of the pimping.

Bear in mind, rather, what Dill says of Lucian: "One cannot help feeling, in reading some of Lucian's pieces, that, man of genius as he was, a man of no age, or a man of all ages, he is looking at human life from far above, with no limitations of time, and passing a judgment which may be repeated in the thirtieth century." There you have it. There you have the difference between merchandise and art. Most of Lucian or Juvenal is as modern today as it was eighteen hundred years ago.

You will find it written by some literary critics that the writer's task is to mirror his own age *for his own age.* On the contrary that is the task for the journalist. Professor Ray B. West, Jr. has written in his *Western Review:* "Granting that the conditions of modern society are not those which an artist would willingly choose, I would still propose that the best he can do is accept them as gracefully as possible. They are, after all, the materials in which the contemporary artist must work; and while the writer is under no compulsion to like them they are all he possesses." Professor West, in my opinion, errs in every statement he makes. Juvenal and Lucian and a thousand other artists did not "gracefully" accept the conditions of their time. Those who accepted them gracefully were those inventing some fresh stimulus for exhausted appetites. The conditions of modern society are certainly not "all the materials" possessed by such artists as Anatole France, Machen, Robert Nathan, Cabell, Mann and many more. Professor West reveals his tastes and attitudes in the matter when, looking for three contemporary novelists whose work may "survive for some time," he puts his finger on Dreiser, Anderson, and Robert Penn Warren. One wonders whether he could understand what Professor Goodenough means by "a spirit over-shadowed in our picture of classic Greece only because of ᴣsence there of the great men who must have been as exceptional and remote then as they would have been at any time since."

It is the artists who are exceptional and remote who

survive, as Lucian has survived, for eighteen or thirty centuries. Those who gracefully accept the conditions of their time and do no more than to mirror their own generation may be remembered for their sociology but not for their art. The greatest artists never belong to their age but to the ages, and the breadth of time which they encompass is one measure of their art. It is their work that is made manifest and tested with fire. Marjorie Brace has said that the writer "cannot write seriously without alienating himself from the values of his society, and at the same time he cannot function apart from his audience." But he can learn to be content with a small audience.

If you come to feel the bitterness that Juvenal felt you may say that if you strive to write for the future as well as for your own time, and fail, you will never know that you failed. That is just as well. That is one blessing that nobody can take from you. Better to die thinking you have failed, as Keats died, and be found, than to die as some of his contemporaries died, convinced that they had written for the ages, only to be forgotten a century later or to be held up to ridicule. After all, your task as an artist is to deliver to mankind the fruits of the talent you were born with. If you do that you may not be long remembered but you will have fought the good fight and kept the faith that Paul spoke of.

I would say that here, as in all other fields, we must give to Caesar those things that are Caesar's and to God those things that are God's. Eschew bitterness and don't fall into the weakness of complaint. In this transition period of tremendous stress and travail, when artists plunge into the dark night of the ocean or walk far out into the sea, never to return; when high government officials leap from windows, and those charged with their death are themselves victims of their own inner turmoil and conflicts; when we have more people in hospitals for the insane than in all other hospitals combined; when the Christian churches are breaking from their moorings and passing into the realm of mythology; when the ancient religion of emperor worship is rising again under dictators to capture and enslave us—when all this is true, popular fiction and all popular art must continue to be one of the principal forms of therapy. Let us then give to Caesar what is Caesar's. But if you feel compelled to give to God what is God's there is still no better way than art, nor any country more in need of it than your own.

'word of the Lord.' " Justin Martyr said, "we worship and love the Word who is from the Unbegotten and Ineffable God." Athenagoras: "God who is the eternal mind had the Logos in Himself, beginning from eternity instinct with Logos." Theophilus: "God having his Logos within, in his bowels, begat him, belching him forth along with his own wisdom before all things." Justin says elsewhere: "Logos appears to have been a second God." As Professor Schmidt puts it, "In the Fourth Gospel the Logos of Philo has become flesh." Rank says: "The lower 'mouth' of the woman, which 'makes' man materially, becomes finally identified with the upper mouth of man from which streams his speech, the Logos." Ah, the vanity of men in their desire to be creators!

Now all this may seem to you to be, and certainly is, mystical and confusing; but this much you need to grasp: the ancient belief in the power of the word, that is, of human speech, became in the hands of later mystics wisdom or knowledge, the power in divinity; and still later in the hands of Hellenizing Christians, Jesus himself. By this process which refined a primitive superstition speech was transformed into deity. Christian theologians dodge this matter, refusing to see it for what it was, though what it was is unmistakably clear. For that matter, the doctrine of God as the Word prevailed, says Carus, "in China, in India, in Persia, in Greece, in ancient Egypt." This religious concept, like many others, was refined as it evolved, quite as the Jews century after century refined and evolved the anthropomorphic deity of Abraham until they got the transcendental God of Philo.

The persistence of the primitive linguistic outlook in the work of the profoundest thinkers! It is a thought to make us pause. Throughout the world, the word is still regarded with superstition, reverence and fear. We have not changed as much as we like to think. For it is true, as Dujardin says, that our institutions, including language, "have their origins in the institutions of our neolithic ancestors, and it is impossible to fathom their meaning without returning to this starting point and tracing their subsequent evolutions." Yes indeed, the past is the present. It is true, as Cohen says, that today "we are using thought-forms belonging to the earliest stages of our culture to express an understanding of the world today . . . the language of man is as full —even fuller—of reminiscences of its ancestry than his physical structure. . . . In some ways the twentieth century suffers more grievously than any previous age from the ravages of verbal superstitions." "Blunders of archaic thought," says Hartland, "on matters that seem perfectly obvious to us have become permanent as a part of the mental equipment of the race." For assistance in this difficult matter we can turn with profit to the ablest works of the semanticists, though with some of those who cherish "the ravages of verbal superstitions" and "blunders of archaic thought" it is popular to hold the semanticists up to ridicule.

But the blunders and ravages are there in overwhelming abundance, and nobody in the world should be more eager to grasp this truth and probe its difficulties and master more adequate thought-forms than the writer himself. Because words are his tool and his only tool.

In ancient times, then, language was magic. So it is still for most people. "I think you are lying," says the Master Philologist to Jurgen. "In any event, justice is a word, and I control all words." And Jurgen says, "There is no weapon like words, no armor against words." Anaitis asks him, "But is it magic?—are you certain that it is authentic magic?" Jurgen: "I have learned that there is always magic in words." Have we all learned that much?—or shall we say that most of the magic has fled? "Language," said Max Müller, "has been called by Jean Paul 'a dictionary of faded metaphors': so it is, and it is the duty of the etymologist to try to restore them to their original brightness." And again he said: "Wherever we analyze language in a truly scholarlike spirit, whether in Iceland or in Tierra del Fuego, we shall find in it the key to some of the deepest secrets of the human mind, and the solution of problems in philosophy and religion which nothing else can supply. Each language, whether Sanscrit or Zulu, is like a palimpsest, which, if carefully handled, will disclose the original text beneath the superficial writing. . . ." To learn how true it is that our words today are a dictionary of faded metaphors, and how superficial it is compared to language of ancient times, you have only to read such a two-volume work as Harold Bayley's *The Lost Language of Symbolism*.

Ancient peoples, and none more than the Jews, believed that what was *written* in their sacred books was truth. Most persons today defer to the written word without ever looking under the palimpsest. Propaganda has become such a deadly and devastating weapon that some intelligent persons accept as gospel the grosser absurdities in communist dialectics; and spell-binding dictators like Hitler hold enormous power over the emotions of a people. A promise to cherish and obey practically constitutes, for some, the act itself. Or consider the practice of taking an oath. It is remarkable that a dictionary of faded metaphors can still be so potent.

We are going to look as sharply and clearly at words as we can, beginning with a statement by Professor Wendell Johnson that "before we can change our language it is essential that we develop a certain kind of attitude toward it—that attitude that language *is to be viewed as a form of behavior* [italics supplied] and that, like other behavior, it is to be evaluated as technique"—not as Logos, not as God, not as tens of thousands of metaphors, not as a mysterious power in itself, independent of the forces around it, but as technique. To see it as technique, as a behavior-pattern, we must of course put aside our prepossessions.

Some twenty years ago I sat in the home of a New York novelist, a woman of unusual intellect and background. We were talking about writers and writing when suddenly she turned to me and asked, "Do you agree with me that the English language is a marvellously subtle and flexible instrument?" I did not agree. Even then I had the unhappy impression that language is not what it should be, though I did not at the time realize that it is indeed many thousands of metaphors so faded that most of the ancient meanings have been lost. I had studied several languages besides my own, but more than that, I had taken courses in the origin, history and evolution of language. I had learned that language evolves in a rather blind and blundering way, without much rhyme or reason; I had not learned that civilization so adulterates it that in countless instances we have only empty words from which the meanings have fled. I felt that language today is a quite obtuse and clumsy and lifeless thing, a view, I am aware, that is rank heresy among some who teach it. But let them read any standard source on ancient symbolisms to see how many words have gone dead on us that we have not been able to restore to life. If we do not talk in metaphor we simply do not communicate the richness and mystery of our world.

I pointed out to this novelist that we have five senses, yet live chiefly by the sense of sight. We have a sense of smell and of taste, both wonderfully developed in ancient times; but what descriptive words do we have to express the infinite

variations in flavor and scent? Only a very few. If you
want to learn how true this is, try to describe any odor so
that one unfamiliar with it can get a good idea of it. I
spent some hours recently in an herb garden and in turn
tasted and smelled marjoram, summer savory, saffron, rose-
mary, thyme, lavender, coriander, and a number of others.
I could not describe their flavors and scents because I have
no words to do it with. I chew some coriander and say, "It
is like— It is a little like—" What? I breathe of violet or
heliotrope or pineapple or melon and say the scent is like—
what? Shall I say that it is sweet, pleasant, fragrant, de-
lightful?

Go through your thesaurus and discover for yourself the
inadequacy of our language, its obtuseness, its vague
approximations.

You want to describe the odor of a great hedge of lilac in
full bloom. You turn to Roget but under what word?
Fragrance? Under fragrance you find aroma, redolence,
incensation, perfume, bouquet, sweet smell, sweet odor, aro-
matic perfume, scent. The next paragraph is comparisons,
and you find agalloch or agallochum, agalwood, eaglewood,
aloeswood, sandalwood, cedar, champak, calambac, and a
dozen more, all useless. The next paragraph names flowers,
including lilac. Possibly you think the odor of lilac is
sweet and you turn to sweet to find: saccharine, melodious,
color, clean, agreeable, lovely! You will be forced to fall
back on impressionism, suggestion, symbol, vagueness,
hoping that your arrangement of words will communicate.

So let's be done, for our own good, with this myth about
the subtlety, versatility and suppleness of language. It is
today an obtuse, illogical and fumbling instrument which
we have inherited from primitive times, and from which
we have lost most of the original richness. You have only
to read and understand the amazing symbolisms in "The
Song of Songs" to realize that. Writers have confessed that
they have sat an hour or half a day without being able to
write a paragraph or even a sentence. That is not at all
surprising. Our mental, and even more, our emotional,
processes *are* subtle, elusive, devious, tenuous, cunning and
often uncapturable. We try to put them into words. It is
much like trying to put the scent of lilac into empty jars.

The worst mythmakers in the world in respect to language
are some of those who teach it. I sat under a number,
including teachers of writing, and every one of them, man

and woman, spoke rapturously to their students of language as a wonderfully strong and delicate tool. It is strong like a sledgehammer and delicate like the odor of cabbage. In my early years of teaching I was guilty of the same unconscious dishonesty. When I think of these former teachers, telling their popeyed students how *subtle* language is, I recall the words of the Autocrat: "The man who is never conscious of a state of feeling or of intellectual effort entirely beyond expression by any form of words whatsoever is a mere creature of language." I'd put it more strongly. I'd say that the inadequacy of language drives writers to the queer things they do, from e. e. cummings to James Joyce. When José Garcia, a poet, was reviewed in *Time* one line was set down as:

> a,living,giant,all,in,little,pieces

A reader said how much improved it would be as:

> a;living;giant;all;in;little;pieces

Or, even better:

> a :living :giant :all :in :little :pieces

But he thought the best way might be:

> a̶,̶l̶i̶v̶i̶n̶g̶,̶g̶i̶a̶n̶t̶,̶a̶l̶l̶,̶i̶n̶,̶l̶i̶t̶t̶l̶e̶,̶p̶i̶e̶c̶e̶s̶

Well, when writers strive with such pains to capture the evanescent, the delicate, the elusive and fail we should be charitable toward their lunacies.

In a blurb before me Clifton Fadiman says that Wolfe had the greatest command of language of anyone in his generation. It is an absurd statement. Those with the greatest *command* of language are certain eminent philologists who, far more than the rest of us, are masters of a dozen languages, of the multitude of relationships among languages, and of the evolution in the meaning of words. With Wolfe it would be closer to the truth to say that language was in command of him. He calls to mind Pater's "lover of words for their own sake, to whom nothing about them is unimportant." Wolfe simply poured Roget into his books. Words for him were so filled with magic that he could not resist them, but opened his creative windows wide to let them all in. Ravished by words, he could not, as Sinclair Lewis once pointed out, choose among six or three adjectives or adverbs but used all of them. They came to him laden with meanings, or, more exactly, suggestions; he found them irresistibly evocative; he loved them, he pounced upon them, he wrote them down. If he had known a dozen languages as well as he knew English he would, I have no doubt, have tried to write simultaneously in all of them. His fondness for *Ulysses* was fully motivated. And it is well to remember at this point that Freud recognized the saving of energy as essential to the enjoyment of wit, and Rank's observation that "the greater the economy the greater the pleasure." Since Fadiman has a reputation as a wit his statement is all the more disconcerting: economy was not one of Wolfe's virtues.

It is well to realize this truth, that we are so much the victims of words that we find it difficult to resist them when they are put before us. In spite of skepticism we must make some response to them. The mere chanting of words, not in meaningful phrases but in senseless abracadabra, has a hypnotizing effect on us, as the ancient exorcists knew well and the auctioneer knows today. Let the professors of writing say that we choose words to express meanings. Much of our time we do nothing of the sort. Words seize us and enter us. When the seizure is violent, as in the case of Wolfe, and too often in the case of most of us, we perceive that words are using the man.

"We are apt," wrote Edward Everett Hale, a professor of rhetoric, "to use indiscriminately words which come pretty near the meaning we have in mind, and so to lose the possibility of exact expression. It is a common vulgarism to use the word *share* as if it meant precisely the same thing as part." Are we to suppose that the professor was there using words *exactly?* It is not clear to me how one can *lose* a possibility. A commentator on Flaubert tells us that the author of *Bovary* was "possessed of an absolute belief that there exists but one way of expressing one thing, one word to call it by, one adjective to qualify, one verb to animate it." Flaubert, we are told, believed that among all the possible forms of expression there was one, if he could find it, that would exactly express what he wanted to say.

As though one can ever know exactly what one wants to say. And what is an absolute belief?

Let's look at Crabbe under *ecstasy:* "Ecstasy, rapture, transport. There is a strong resemblance in the meaning and application of these words. They all express an extraordinary elevation of the spirit or an excessive tension of the mind." Ecstasy, we are informed, benumbs the faculties and often takes away the power of speech and thought; but where do you find it used in that sense? Rapture "invigorates the powers and calls them into action." Transports are "sudden bursts of passion which, from their vehemence, may lead to intemperate actions." Will a reprieve from sentence of death produce in the person ecstasy, rapture or transport? Ecstasy, we are told. Will a devout person contemplating a holy object feel transport, rapture or ecstasy? Rapture, Mr. Crabbe says. Go through a book of prose or poetry by any eminent author and observe for yourself whether he pays attention to Crabbe and Hale.

Meredith's Mrs. Mountstuart came closer to the practic if not to Fowler. "Like all rapid phrasers," her author tel us, "she detested the analysis of her sentence. It had ı outline in vagueness, and was flung out to be apprehend ı, not dissected." In the so-called exact sciences there may e exactness in the use of words. When we come over to he social sciences, and from there to creative writing, w re in the company of the Mrs. Mountstuarts.

That is so because most words have as many sha s of meaning as there are persons who use them. We who rite are only vaguely apprehended, possibly because o own apprehensions are only vague at best. In the cas f all abstract words there is no exact meaning. You n determine this truth for yourself by asking your iterate friends to define such terms as beauty, truth, odness, holiness, honesty, conscience, soul, morality—o ecstasy, rapture and transport. If you find two who prec ely agree on the definition of any abstract word you will ı ve reason to be amazed. The meanings of words for us are etermined loosely, vaguely, clumsily by our experiences and so it follows that the more dissimilar our experie es the less likely we are to agree.

Words are our tyrants and masters. The ıder is that we are able to communicate as well as we Or do we? Certainly the condition of the world does n ncourage us to think so. Persons as astute as the mem s of our Department of State took a long time to learn that the Russians were not using the word democracy as they used it. Go back to Johnson's statement that language is behavior and you will understand why that was so.

Many experiments with college students have revealed this, that they can read a simple paragraph of prose and reread it a half-dozen times and still not be able to abstract its meaning well enough to set it down. That is so not only because they are not trained to see what they look at; many words for them have no specific meaning. Yet we do persist in the quaint belief that when we speak and write we are understood. There is no more lugubrious assumption in American education than that when the professor talks his students understand him.

For one thing the meanings of many words are not clear to those of us who use them. We live in an atmosphere of vague suggestions, of rough approximations, which we take to be meanings, upon which we have general apprehension and agreement. We take an awful lot for granted. Just above I used the word lugubrious. I have observed that for many persons it means funny or silly or ridiculous. The dictionary says it comes from the Latin meaning to mourn, and means mournful or doleful. If you were to say, as many do, "I believe in the Golden Rule," no doubt you would expect to be understood. But do you yourself know what you mean? What actually *do* you mean when you say you believe in religion or in God? Of religion there are ten thousand printed definitions, and of God I should think almost as many.

Let us now consider another aspect of the matter. Many words become obsolete and are abandoned; most of them continuously change their meaning, or, as in many instances, take on new meanings, and so come at last to mean any one of a half-dozen or a dozen different things. Such as the word *nice*. In a book by Lorge we are told that the word *by* has forty-one meanings; that *open* can mean uncovered, or not closed, or unrestricted, or forthright, or not frozen. *Run* and its compounds have eight hundred meanings; and *put, pass, stand, work* and *make* all have hundreds. What is a *man?* Lorge says there are twenty different meanings for this word.

We use a lot of words that no longer have much meaning, if any at all. Soul (though I use it throughout this book) is one, heaven is another. Of words that have completely

lost their original meaning and now have none at all take
proper names. Among the ancient Hebrews Caleb meant
dog; Rachel, ewe; Adam, red earth; Eve, life or possibly
the womb of life. Leah was the weary one, Lilith the one
belonging to darkness, Mary or Miriam, from myrrh, the
bitter one. Benjamin was the son of the right stone
(daughters came from the left, or weaker!) ; Gabriel was
a man of God; Jeshua—Joshua—Jesus was the one who
saved. With the other ancients the matter was the same.
Cynthia was the moon, Fulvia the yellow-haired, Hypatia
the highest, Livia the frivolous, Marcia the daughter of
Mars, and Myrtle was the myrtle. Andrew was the manly
one, Peter was the rock, George was the farmer, Mark was
the warrior, and Pastor was the guardian of souls. Today
the names of persons are merely words.

More important because more difficult to use than those
which have lost their meaning are those which have gathered
many meanings. If in a story you write, "She was a nice
person," are you just flinging out a word to be apprehended?
Or do you mean that she was fastidious; or affected coy
reserve; or was discriminating; or was merely pleasant?
If you write, "He was a religious person" do you mean that
he believed in a supreme being, or faithfully observed the
dogmas of his church, or strove to love his neighbor as
himself? If you write, "She was a beautiful woman" do
you mean in her physical appearance in accordance with
your idea of beauty or with certain standards in aesthetics;
and, if either of those, do you mean that her face and figure
were attractive, or that her personality was informed with
grace and kindliness? Or do you mean that she was a
glamour type in vogue at the moment? What do you expect
your reader to think you meant?

Well, most writing, like the lady's sentence, is flung at us.
Since meanings are elusive and uncertain things, since
language is indeed a form of behavior, with its pattern
varying from person to person, and since so few persons
ever pause to reflect on the meanings of the words they use
or to realize that the meanings for them, if these do exist
with any exactness, are not necessarily what the meanings
may be for another, *can* writing be much more than words
flung at readers? Should the ideal be Wolfe or Flaubert?
Should you pour the dictionary into your stories and trust
to magic or should you try to determine exactly what you
mean? Or should you fall back on impressionism, which

a critic once defined as a skeleton on which there hangs an effect?

You will of course answer the question according to what you are. In an effort to bring home to you the slippery nature of word-magic, I shall now open at random some books on a shelf before me and look at a sentence here and there, choosing only simple ones with commonplace words.

Edward Carpenter asks: "Which of us has ever really seen a tree?" There is a question of nine simple words. Do we understand it? None of us has ever seen a tree in the sense in which Carpenter used the word. For primitive peoples a tree was a great deal more than the appearance which we see. It was a house of God, a phallic symbol, a miracle standing in the earth-womb, an act of divine creation, a living, breathing thing with speech, powers and spirit. It may be a pity that a tree means so little to us today, the carburetor on a car so much.

Rank says: "Truth is what I believe or affirm, doubt is denial or rejection." What do you mean by the word truth? something fixed and unalterable, or only the subjective reality of appearance? Is the truth of sin the dogma of original depravity, or the social evils arbitrarily determined by people at any moment of history? The third definition of truth in my dictionary says, conformity to fact or reality. Under *reality* I find: that which is real!

I open next Dr. Chideckel's *Female Sex Perversion:* "Normal women live and sleep together, and to them the discussion of sex perversities are [*sic*] repellent. Most of them do not even know that such things could be possible. Two girls seen together are sure to be normals. The homosexual walks alone. A woman by herself in public where she should normally have a companion is bound to arouse suspicion of some kind. Usually that suspicion is justified." Astonished, one turns to the title-page and the blurbs. This man has a reputation abroad; his book was produced in this country by the Eugenics Publishing Company and carries a foreword by a member of the Johns Hopkins medical faculty. Yet it is plain enough that if he means what his words seem to say he is preposterous.

I open Sumner: "A man in debt is not free. A man who has made a contract is not free. A man who has contracted duties and obligations as husband and father, or has been born into them as a citizen, son, brother, etc., is not free." Did you imagine that you knew what the simple word free means? I open the dictionary and find twelve definitions. The third says that a free person or thing is one "not subject to some particular authority, obligation or restriction." In that sense nothing under the sun is free. Yet in a contemporary novel before me is the sentence: "He was a free man in a free country." What did the author mean? In all honesty we have to say that we don't know and that probably he did not know either. What *did* Roosevelt mean by the four freedoms?

I open Davenport's *Primitive Traits in Religious Revivals* and look for a simple sentence: "Clear thinking and emotion are now true comrades in religion." What does *clear* mean? My dictionary gives seven definitions, as well as various subdivisions. Clear means free of anything that dims and blurs; or free from contamination; or something distinctly seen, heard or understood; or the ability to perceive distinctly and keenly; or free from doubt; or free from guile; or free from burden or limitation. What did Davenport mean? I've no idea. It is going far to say that there is *clear* thinking or *clear* emotion.

I open Rudolf Flesch's book *The Art of Plain Talk*, which drew cheers from writers, college presidents and advertising agencies. "I cannot imagine anybody doing any rewriting and simplifying without realizing that language is, at best, a crude and arbitrary system of symbols and that we cannot understand anything as long as we mistake words for things. This kind of error is the source of most prejudices and irrational arguments." On the whole we must agree with that, though Flesch, with his mania for simplifying, for making all things apprehensible to the eighth-grade mentality, fails to note that understanding sometimes places great demands upon intelligence and knowledge. Here are a few instances, the first from Lippert:

"If to the savage in his intellectual isolation a soul seems to be the cause behind every phenomenon, then, in the natural development of thought, to a philosopher, whose intellectual horizon has expanded to comprehend the idea of a universe, the cause of all causes behind this universe must seem to be a universal soul. From this idea, so evidently derived from the domain of the cult, philosophizing humanity has never since been able to extricate itself."

Then from Gumplowicz, another great sociologist: "Every code of human morals from the earliest times to the present day has this thoroughly characteristic peculiarity: the

product of actual occurrences and real relations is everywhere explained by and derived from imaginary circumstances, and men cannot comprehend a moral idea otherwise."

And then to Frazer who said that the "publication of
the Deuteronomic Code in written form [3rd cen., B.C.]
marked an era in the history not only of the Jewish people
but of humanity. It was the first step toward the canoni-
zation of Scripture and thereby to the substitution of the
written for the spoken word as the supreme and infallible
rule of conduct. The accomplishment of the process by the
completion of the Canon in the succeeding centuries laid
thought under shackles from which in the Western world
it has never since wholly succeeded in emancipating itself."

We see that those three thoughts are closely related.
What they mean to any reader must depend, not on Mr.
Flesch's simplification of the sentences, but on prepossess-
sions, knowledge and capacity for thought. Anyone who
has grasped the profound and self-evident conclusions given
there by three great men of the past has grasped, I should
think, the essentials of a liberal education.

Let's add to those two more. The first is from Leuba:
"The evils bred by the traditional conception of God may
be called by the general name 'other worldliness.' It would
be difficult to evaluate the harm done to humanity in the
past by the conviction that the real destination of man is the
World to Come, and equally difficult to estimate the harm
done by the conviction that for its ethical improvement
society is dependent upon a personal God."

And now from Lecky: "Nothing can be more certain to
an attentive observer, than that the great majority even of
those who reason much about their opinions have arrived
at their conclusions by a process quite distinct from reasoning. They may be perfectly unconscious of the fact, but
the ascendency of old associations is upon them; and, in the
overwhelming majority of cases, men of the most various
creeds conclude their investigations by simply acquiescing
in the opinions they have been taught. . . . The number
of persons who have a rational basis for their belief is
probably infinitesimal; for illegitimate influences not only
determine the convictions of those who do not examine,
but usually give a dominating bias to the reasonings of
those who do."

In those five instances we have thinking just about as

clear, just about as lucid, as we can find it anywhere in this world. With all of them in mind, but particularly Lecky, let us now glance at a few statements "quite distinct from reasoning," where the ascendency of old associations produces acquiescence. Wayland, *Elements of Moral Science:* "That is always the most happy condition of a nation, and that nation is most accurately obeying the laws of our constitution, in which the number of the human race is most rapidly increasing. Now it is certain that under the law of chastity, that is, when individuals are exclusively united to each other, the increase of population will be more rapid than under any other circumstances."

Bentham, *Springs of Action:* "As there is not any sort of pleasure that is not itself a good, nor any sort of pain the exemption from which is not a good, and as nothing but the expectation of the eventual enjoyment of pleasure in some shape, or of exemption from pain in some shape, can operate in the character of a motive, a necessary consequence is that if by motive he meant *sort* of motive, there is not any such thing as a bad motive."

Canon C. T. P. Grierson: "The widespread belief of the early Church in the virgin birth can be reasonably accounted for only by the occurrence of the fact itself." Practically all the gods in ancient myth were virgin-born! A. W. F. Blunt, Fellow of Exeter College, Oxford: "The interpretation of a dream 'belongs to God'; the question whether its message is a divine communication or not must ultimately be answered by an appeal to the religious consciousness, or in other words to the higher reason."

Now to Leon Gautier's history of French epic poetry: "Represent to yourselves the first man at the moment when he issues from the hand of God, when his vision rests for the first time upon his new empire. Imagine, if it be possible, the exceeding vividness of his impressions when the magnificence of the world is reflected in the mirror of his soul. Intoxicated, almost mad with admiration, gratitude, and love, he raises his eyes to heaven, not satisfied with the spectacle of the earth; then discovering God in the heavens, and attributing to him all the honor of this magnificence and of the harmonies of creation, he opens his mouth, the first stammerings of speech escape his lips—he speaks; ah, no, he sings, and the first song of the lord of creation will be a hymn to God his creator."

This chapter has tried to suggest to you a few of the

essentials in good writing. Possibly they come down to this: an understanding of language as a magical but crude and obtuse instrument, burdened with a multitude of associations, most of them now not only useless but dangerous, from our primitive past; and a need to make your thought as clear as you can make it. Remember that the meanings of the words you write will be defined not by you but by the one who reads them, and that the power of abstracting *your* meaning, taken for granted by our schools, exists at a low level in most people. Words are your difficult and elusive tool. It is easy to use the tool carelessly and loosely; it is hard to use it with much exactness, even if you know with exactness what you want to say. Words can easily become your master. You can never master them. Mastery would be great art but that kind of art no man has yet written.

CHARACTER

"If people are at all peculiar in character they
have to suffer from the very rules that produce
comfort in others."—HARDY

"It would almost appear that man is exclusively
imaginative and poetical; and that his mate, the
fair, the graceful, the bewitching, with the sweetest
and purest of natures, cannot help being something
of a groveller."—MEREDITH

"A woman if she have the misfortune of knowing
anything should conceal it as well as she can."
—JANE AUSTEN

Because seeing themselves for what they are has been
the last thing in the world that all but a few people have
wanted to do, we find human nature insulated with the
self-protective assumptions. It is generally assumed, for
instance, that people by nature are honest, kind, truthful,
loyal, compassionate and merciful, but *by nature* they are
none of these things. In a news magazine there recently
appeared a frank confession by Al Capp, a comic strip
artist. "All comedy," says Capp, "is based on man's delight
in man's inhumanity to man." With that formula "I have
made forty million people laugh more or less every day for
sixteen years." These people are not "heartless wretches"
but "normal human beings."

Very well. The young writer who wishes to be a serious
artist, who has his eye on the next centuries as well as on
his own, must strive to see human beings for what they
are, without their halo of myth. For we can be reasonably
sure of this, that somewhere in the future, after the research is completed and the evidence is in, human nature
will be clearly seen for what it is. The artist tries to an-
ticipate the future. For all his trying he may not be able
to see people as clearly as they will some day be seen but
he can hope to see them much more truly than most of his
fellows see them. He can at least grasp such basic truths

as that stated by Israel Abrahams, that "virtues are more attainable than virtue, characteristics than character." Or the observation of Rivarol who, viewing the French Revolution, said that the "most civilized empires are as close to barbarism as the most polished steel is to rust; nations like metals shine only on the surface." He can understand that most human behavior is "determined by an extremely low order of self-interest." He has only to study the endorsements in advertising to grasp that much, or to contemplate what Nock designated as Epstean's Law, that if self-preservation is the first law of life, exploitation is the second.

He can perceive with Cabell that this race in "its entirety, in the whole outcome of its achievement [is] beyond all wording petty and ineffectual." Nevertheless "still I believe life to be a personal transaction between myself and Omnipotence; I believe that what I do is somehow of importance; and I believe that I am on a journey toward some very public triumph." We may have to accept the "dynamic illusion" or all go mad but it does not follow that we have to let the illusion engulf us.

What is man?

"What is man?" asked Pepin, Charlemagne's eldest son. "The slave of death, the guest of an inn, a wayfarer passing." "How strange a thing is man!" said Peter Damian. "But half a cubit of him, and a universe full of material things will not satisfy it!"

What is man?

"This," wrote Wolfe, "is man: for the most part a foul, wretched, abominable creature, a packet of decay, a bundle of degenerating tissues, a creature that gets old and hairless and has a foul breath, a hater of his kind, a cheater, a scorner, a mocker, a reviler, a thing that kills and murders in a mob or in the dark, loud and full of brag surrounded by his fellows, but without the courage of a rat alone. . . . This is man, who will steal his friend's woman, feel the leg of his host's wife below the table cloth, dump fortunes on whores, bow down in worship before charlatans, and let his poets die. . . . Yes, this is man, and it is impossible to say the worst of him, for the record of his obscene existence, his baseness, lust, cruelty, and treachery, is illimitable. . . . This is man, who, if he can remember ten golden moments of joy and happiness out of all his years, ten moments unmarked by care, unseamed by aches and itches, has power to lift himself with his expiring breath and say: 'I have lived upon this earth and known glory! . . .' This is man, and one wonders why he wants to live at all."

"So it is," wrote Cabell in his wise book, "that the accepted routine of life's conduct tends to make mountebanks of us inevitably: and the laborious years weave small hypocrisies like cobwebs about our every action, and at last about our every thought. The one consoling feature is that we are so incessantly busied at concealment of our personal ignorance and incapacity as to lack time to detect one another. For we are all about the arduous task: at every moment of our lives we who are civilized persons must regard, if we indeed do not submit to be controlled by, that which is expected of us: and we are harassed always by an instant need of mimicking the natural behavior of men as, according to our generally received if erroneous standards, 'men ought to be.' "

"I do not think," wrote Maugham, "that I am any better or any worse than most people, but I do know that if I set down every action in my life and every thought that has crossed my mind the world would consider me a monster of depravity." "We are so degraded," wrote Thoreau, "that we cannot speak simply of the necessary functions of human nature." "In our friend's misfortunes," said de Rochefoucault, "there's something secretly pleasant to us." "If you wish to win a man's heart," said Disraeli, "allow him to confute you."

"After infinite travail," wrote Balfour in *Foundations of Belief*, "there has evolved a race with conscience enough to know that it is vile, and intelligence enough to know that it is insignificant. We survey the past, and see that its history is of blood and tears, of helpless blundering, of wild revolt, of stupid acquiescence, of empty aspirations." Ah yes, cried de Maupassant, "we shall ever continue to be borne down by the old and odious customs, the criminal prejudices, the ferocious ideas, of our barbarous forefathers, for we are but animals and we shall remain animals, led only by the instincts that nothing will ever change." "The life of man," said Spengler in *Man and Technics*, "is the life of a brave and splendid, cruel and cunning beast of prey. He lives by catching, killing and consuming." "Humanity, what is it," asked George Moore, "but a pigsty where liars, hypocrites, and the obscene in spirit congregate; it has been so since the great Jew conceived it, and it will be so till the end."

But is that all of it? Is there also, as Lowell said, a "rooted instinct in men to admire what is better and more beautiful than themselves"? Of how many can we say, as Chesterton said of Dickens, that "he disliked a certain look on the face of a man when he looks down on another man. And that look on that face is the only thing in the world that we have really to fight between here and the fires of hell"? Did Montaigne express *all* of it when he said that "the laws of conscience, which we pretend to be derived from nature, proceed from custom"? Did Bishop Wilson express all of it when he said that virtue is "hardly distinguishable from a kind of sensuality"? If that is all of it, should we then portray human nature for what it is? No, said Meredith, for it is "unwholesome for men and women to see themselves as they are." We must preserve the dynamic illusion, said Cabell; we must portray human nature not as it is but as it ought to be. To all of which I would say that it is not *by nature* half so vile as it seems to be everywhere: we have not yet tried to understand what perversions of purpose and will have been created in us by nineteen centuries of the doctrine of original depravity.

But it is true that all these writers and a host of others who have written in similar vein have not too grossly exaggerated the matter. The records of the past are there and the more one reads them the more one is appalled. Still, there is another side of it. We have a human race that has almost lost itself in the multifarious and complex labyrinths of its mythmaking, that has so lost itself indeed that it has yet to learn that the source of evil is not in us but in our ignorance. "I conceive," said Peacock's Foster, "that men are virtuous in proportion as they are enlightened; and that, as every generation increases in knowledge, it also increases in virtue." *That* the records of the past also establish as a fact. But our trouble lies in this, that though generation by generation we increase in knowledge we still resist with all our powers the overthrow of certain odious doctrines about ourselves. Look back, for instance, to Mr. W. H. Auden, returning to the doctrine of original sin! As civilization brings with it its own diseases which threaten to destroy it, so increase of knowledge of ourselves is met at every turn by more desperate efforts to rationalize the knowledge and make it serve our sentiment of self-regard. As the ancients allegorized their legends to make them acceptable to a more enlightened time; as the Jews struggled to find in Abraham's anthropomorphic god a subtle and hidden meaning, being unwilling to accept the literal truth; as the early Christians, faced with the scorn of the Gnostics, who argued that the Old Testament deity was cruel, barbarous and second-rate, strove to find concealed meanings in the offensive biblical passages, so we today try to obscure, embellish and glorify ourselves. The great mass of the people today resist with angry outcry those truths which knowledge puts before them, for no reason but this, that the written word set down by primitive minds contradicts those truths; and among none is the resistance more violent, ridiculous and often infantile than among certain artists, as we shall see in these pages.

I am speaking to young writers. How much of the truth about human nature are you resisting? "The weakness of humanity," said Radcliffe, "is never willingly perceived by young minds." Do you hold with Leopardi that it is life among men, not philosophy, which inspires hatred of men? —or with Sherwood Anderson, that in war we do not kill the man we hate but try to kill the thing we hate in ourselves? Do you hold with Al Capp that his forty million readers delight in cruelty because they are "full of self-doubt, full of desperate need to be reassured"? Would you accept the words of Jurgen?—"I am fettered by cowardice, I am enfeebled by disastrous memories; and I am maimed by old follies. Still, I seem to detect in myself something which is permanent and rather fine."

Ignorance is the blight upon that something that probably could be fine and permanent. Nothing so quickly and deeply offends a person as a remark which undershoots, not the opinion of himself that he would have developed without the distortions of myth, but the false opinion which these have given him. It is not that he is convinced that he is what he believes himself to be. It is that he does not want to face the error in self-judgment if it is there. The subject for him is so unpleasant that he will hate you if you force it on his attention. He will shy away from all books that try to prod him into self-knowledge; for the symptom, let me repeat, is the patient's friend, his modern guardian angel and *genius*. The strange thing about him is that while resisting knowledge of self he will continue to accept certain dogmas from ancient times that declare him to be vile.

This resistance we can observe in its most depressing form if we look at some autobiographical novels; because in most of these the authors, far from representing themselves as they were, exalt and glorify themselves. I take first a passage from Wolfe, on which I have yet to find an incredulous word in print.

"Lying darkly in his crib, washed, powdered, and fed, he thought quietly of many things before he dropped off to sleep. . . . At these moments he was heartsick with weary horror as he thought of the discomfort, weakness, dumbness, the infinite misunderstanding he would have to endure before he gained even physical freedom. He grew sick as he thought of the weary distance before him, the lack of co-ordination of the centres of control, the undisciplined and rowdy bladder, the helpless exhibition he was forced to give in the company of his sniggering, pawing brothers and sisters."

You perceive, I hope, that we are here viewing the most remarkable infant in all of recorded history. He is shamed because he cannot control his bladder; he is heartsick because he is not able to wash and powder himself; he is appalled by thought of the long lifetime ahead of him. Even more:

"He was in agony because he was poverty-stricken in symbols: his mind was caught in a net because he had no words to work with. He had not even names for the objects around him. . . . He wondered savagely how they would feel if they knew what he really thought: at other times he had to laugh at them and their whole preposterous comedy of errors as they pranced around for his amusement. . . . The situation was at once profoundly annoying and comic . . . hearing their voices become absurd and sentimental whenever they addressed him, speaking to him words which he did not yet understand, but which he saw they were mangling in the preposterous hope of rendering intelligible that which has been previously mutilated, he had to laugh at the fools in spite of his vexation." After the relatives went away leaving him in a shuttered room, this babe "saw his life down the solemn vista of a forest aisle, and he knew that he would always be the sad one." He knew that "he must always walk down lonely passages." He saw himself as "an inarticulate stranger, an amusing little clown" and his "brain went black with terror."

A more preposterous—to use Wolfe's favorite word there

—passage probably cannot be found in all serious literature; but even so, it is typical of countless pages in the Wolfe novels which so over-glorify the author-protagonist that we cannot accept him as a human being at all, but only as a ridiculous image of the well-beloved. Hardly less astonishing than Wolfe's failure to grasp the simple realities is that of the persons who reviewed him. We don't know whether to be more amazed at Wolfe, who could write such drivel, or at reviewers, who accepted it as plausible, or at Maxwell Perkins, who did not throw it out. We are pretty far gone in the self-protective assumptions when without protest or a sense of the incongruous we admit to the mind of the infant the reflections of the man.

We'll now glance at another autobiographical novel, Lewisohn's *The Case of Mr. Crump,* to which we shall return on a later page. The blurbs before me say that this book is generally regarded as Lewisohn's best.

Assumed to be the story of his first unhappy marriage, it has two principal characters, Herbert and his wife Anne, twenty years his senior. Herbert is portrayed throughout as a remarkable musician and man—sensitive, idealistic, proud, compassionate, generous; and his wife as a hellcat, a shrew, a bitch, a vampire with a wish to destroy him. Here, as in all novels of this sort, in which the author is trying to justify, even to glorify, his own acts, we are asked to bleed with the hero and to loathe the nemesis; but the novel does not win for the hero the sympathy of the knowing reader because all the cards are so plainly stacked in his favor. The literate reader must feel that if he was idiot enough to put up year after year with such incredible tyranny and abuse he got about what he deserved. As represented he is hardly a man at all, but a whining and self-pitying weakling, tied to his parents, his race, and enslaved by a romantic idealism. That is all right; there are such men. But it is their author's task to reveal them for what they are. We are told that twice with all the strength he had Herbert struck her full on the mouth, though she was a frail and sickly person. We can hardly believe on the one hand in his nobility if, on the other—and I quote: "fully, brutally, with all his force he struck her across the mouth." As she comes alive to us, page by page, Anne is less the bitch than a pitiable, obsessed and half-insane creature. The characterization of Herbert simply doesn't come off. Mr. Lewisohn was much too close to his materials

—one reviewer says the book was written in white-hot anger. The only thing one should write about oneself in white-hot anger is what one doesn't want anybody to read.

Without apology I shall now say a word about my own autobiographical story. It may be that, eschewing self-glorification and the romantic illusions, I went to the other extreme, and represented Vridar as a worse oaf and weakling than he actually was. In any case I won little sympathy for him. Mr. John Chamberlain said that he wanted to hurl the book through a window, and quite possibly he did; Mr. Joseph Henry Jackson publicly washed his hands of it and of me; and a New York poet, to be mentioned later, cried hotly, with an exclamation point, that life is not like that. A critic, trying to explain why these novels aroused so much resentment and anger, put his finger on it when he said that the reader cannot identify himself with Vridar and his problems because he cannot sufficiently admire him. (Or himself as projected into him!) Very well, I'll rest the case on that. A person like Eugene Gant or Herbert or Vridar, with his sickly idealism, his maudlin and morbid self-pity, his ignorance and egomania and arrogance, is simply *not* admirable; and when the author represents him to be so he departs from the realities and the truths. That may be all right for his sentimental and self-pitying contemporaries with their unwillingness to look at human nature for what it is but we can be sure that posterity will have a different opinion. The basic fallacy here can be found again and again in reviews of fiction. From *Tomorrow* (Feb., 1950) I lift this sentence: "The author obviously has little affection for his chief characters and the result is that he is much more successful with his atmosphere than he is with his people." You may assume that he has affection for his atmosphere; or you may assume that the critic simply doesn't like people in books in whom he cannot see his own largely imaginary virtues. We must dismiss such nonsense by saying that affection in the author for his characters does not necessarily have anything to do with art. Indeed, if the affection is revealed, the *art* will be less.

We are dealing here with what Ruskin called the pathetic fallacy. Pathetic fallacy consists in giving to a situation more emotional content and values than it has the dignity to support. We need not go as far into impatience as St. John Ervine when he exclaimed of Galsworthy: "I imagine that when Mr. Galsworthy goes into a garden, his delight in it is dashed by the thought that somewhere near at hand a thrush is killing a snail"—or a cat a thrush, he might have said. We may even cast a mildly incredulous look at Mr. Albert Schweitzer who, as reported in the American press, is so sensitive in these matters that he will not swat a mosquito or cut down a tree. We need not press the matter to that extreme where the awful gulf between empathy and the cold realities of life leaves us no choice between God and the Devil. Neither on the other hand can we imagine that obvious departure from the realities, when the work is offered as realism, can be viewed as art. You can find a lesson here by comparing what some of her contemporaries thought about the death of Little Nell to what some critics have said about it in more recent times.

"The temperament which admits the pathetic fallacy," said Ruskin, "is that of a mind and body in some sort too weak to deal fully with what is before them or upon them; borne away, or over-clouded, or over-dazzled by emotion; and it is a more or less noble state, according to the force of the emotion which has induced it. For it is no credit to a man that he is not morbid or inaccurate in his perceptions, *when he has no strength of feeling to warp them;* and it is in general a sign of higher capacity and stand in the ranks of being, that the emotions should be strong enough to vanquish, partly, the intellect, and *make it believe what they choose.* But it is still a grander condition when the intellect also rises, till it is strong enough to assert its rule against, or together with, the utmost effort of the passions; and the whole man stands in an iron glow, white-hot, perhaps, but still strong, and in nowise evaporating; even if he melts, losing none of his weight."

"We have three ranks," he says: "the man who perceives rightly, because he does not feel, and to whom the primrose is very accurately the primrose, because he does not love it. Then, secondly, the man who perceives wrongly, because he feels, and to whom the primrose is anything else than a primrose: a star, or a sun, or a fairy's shield, or a forsaken maiden. And then, lastly, there is the man who perceives rightly in spite of his feelings, and to whom the primrose is forever nothing else than itself." A little later he gives us four classes: "the men who feel nothing, and therefore see truly; the men who feel strongly, think weakly, and see untruly (second order of poets) ; the men who feel strongly, think strongly, and see truly (first order of poets) ; and the

men who, strong as human creatures can be, are yet sub-
mitted to influences stronger than they, and see in a sort
untruly, because what they see is inconceivably above them."

The distinctions may be too nicely drawn; they are those
halfway stops to truths, of which Meredith somewhere
speaks. But I think that in general we may accept them,
and I call attention to those words which I have italicized.

Ruskin, as you know, gave instances of what he called
pathetic fallacy. Of Oliver Wendell Holmes'

> The spendthrift crocus, bursting through the mould
> Naked and shivering, with his cup of gold

he says that the crocus is not a spendthrift, that its gold
is not yellow but saffron. Of Kingsley's

> They rowed her across the rolling foam—
> The cruel, crawling foam

that the foam "is not cruel, neither does it crawl." Of
Coleridge's

> The one red leaf, the last of its clan,
> That dances as often as dance it can

that the author has a "morbid, that is to say, a so far false,
idea about the leaf; he fancies a life in it, and will, which
there are not."

In his famous preface to *The Crown of Wild Olive* Ruskin
rhapsodizes over the waters in southern England, saying
"No clearer or diviner waters ever sang with constant lips"
—and so is guilty of what he so vigorously censured in
others. But there is no need to press the matter furthe
I am trying to assume here that "tone of tentative inquir
of which Arnold speaks, "which befits a being of di
faculties and bounded knowledge." What Ruskin object
to is that irrepressible tendency in all of us toward animis   ;
but out of animism have come, the authorities tell us,   ie
religions. Has any of us ever seen a tree, Carpenter '   s,
and it seems plain that Ruskin had not.

The great truth which he puts before us is not that   ad
leaves should not be sad or that a crocus should not   ver
or that waters should not sing with constant lips   hey
will do these things as long as human beings feel   ship
with the world around them. What Ruskin had in   d is

really something else. Because all of us, with Robinson's
Flammonde, have a dark hill to climb; because life is tragic;
because we are lonely—O lost, and by the wind-driven,
ghost—we fall easily into that self-pity which sinks us
deep into bathos. Our emotions too often do force us to
believe those things which loneliness compels us to seek.
We do too commonly have the strength of feeling to warp
ideas, to make a wretched and unrecognizable thing of
truth, to disguise and distort and even to deny reality in
our efforts to come to and preserve peace of mind.

The young artist is on more dangerous ground here than
any other because his emotions are stronger, his egoism is
more unappeased, his sensibilities are more vulnerable, his
vanities are more insatiable. It is easy for him to be defeated by his excesses, as one can observe in the field of
poetry, with its miscarriages and abortions. Too infre-
quently the whole man stands in the iron glow, emotion and
intellect fused.

For one thing, we don't know much about human nature.
Even the greatest psychologists bicker among themselves,
challenging and disputing, and failing to agree on some of
the most general points. Schweitzer in his psychiatric
study of Jesus says that "to form a judgment about any
person on the sole basis of his acts is contrary to all
psychiatric practice and always has something suspicious
about it." Most fiction, then, falls under suspicion. There
was a time when novelists had the right to editorialize and
took full advantage of it. Cut the editorializing out of most
of the important British novels between Defoe and Wells
and you would reduce them by a third. The editorializing
is the brilliant substance of Meredith's *Egoist,* and certainly
no reader would wish to reject Thackeray's comments, even
though he may find Hardy's dull. But today, and particularly in this country, critics jump on a writer if he dares
to offer editorial comment. Now and then there is an exception. Steinbeck's editorial comments seem to have won
approval, possibly because they agreed with popular sentiments of the moment. This prejudice against editorializing
is, it seems to me, a great pity. The full-length study of
an egoist which Meredith made rests not "on the sole basis
of his acts" but on the author's verbal surgery. It is so
with George Eliot's character studies, though after a remarkable analysis of Arthur Donnithorne she concludes:

"I dare not assert that it was not so. The human soul is a very complex thing."

Cabell makes a shrewd point, though as usual with his tongue in his cheek, when he declares that "realists" cannot portray character: "to make a complete and fairminded analysis of any human being, as 'realists' affect to do, is forthwith to avoid any conceivable viewpoint: since our acquaintances, to whom alone we are impartial, we do not take the trouble to analyze, and to our intimates, with whom alone we are familiar, we can by no possibility remain impartial. You would thus no more think of inquiring into your grocer's reasons for turning Methodist than of abhorring your brother because he happened to have murdered somebody. . . . That much-cried-up volume, Madame Bovary, for example, is doubtless a painstaking delineation of a sort of a somebody, which nobody can take oath to be a woman. For, inasmuch as this deplorable Emma is studied with an intimacy and an aloofness of feeling which in human life cannot coexist in an observer, you have no data whereby to judge the portrait's verisimilitude."

A great deal has been written about brilliant analysis and portrayal of character in books (including some of my own) which does not stand close scrutiny. For instance, a critic has said of Henry James's Strether that the author "knows all that is to be known" about him, an opinion that psychologists would find absurd. As another instance let us take what a critic has said about Hemingway.

He tells us that the sixteen principal characters in *For Whom the Bell Tolls* have "three solid dimensions and are more absolutely memorable than the characters of any contemporary American novel, with the possible exception of *The Grapes of Wrath*." Now in both novels we have chiefly fairly simple extroverts, which is to say, persons whose depth of consciousness is shallow. This critic writes of what he calls Hemingway's "fifth dimension," declaring that in one of his short stories "more perhaps than in any other writing, Hemingway got the 'fourth and fifth dimension' of prose, which speaks simultaneously on several levels and whose effect is to leave us aware of an experience at once more real than reality, and with overtones that can only be called extra-natural, of this world and beyond it." That is what someone has called rhapsodizing over the intimation of a shadow on an invisible leaf in the dark.

The truth, when we put aside the nonsense, is that char-